HOW TO
Survive a
DEPOSITION

HOW TO
Survive a
DEPOSITION

Stuart B. Shapiro

Edited by Mark Siegel, Ph.D.

John Wiley & Sons, Inc.
New York ▲ Chichester ▲ Brisbane ▲ Toronto ▲ Singapore

Library of Congress Cataloging-in-Publication Data:
Shapiro, Stuart B.
    How to survive a deposition / Stuart B. Shapiro ; edited by Mark
Siegel.
        p.   cm.
    Includes index.
    ISBN 0-471-00212-7
    1. Depositions—United States. I. Siegel, Mark Richard.
  II. Title.
  KF8900.S494 1994
  347.73'72—dc20
  [347.30772]   93-29659

This book is dedicated to the memory of Robert M. Kiebala, Esq., a superb litigator and a fine human being.

CAVEAT

The law can be like one of those little lizards that's capable of tearing itself away and scampering off to grow a new tail. You may think that you have a firm hold on the critter, but it can be pretty tricky. There's only one way to be sure that you aren't left holding onto the useless tail of the law. Consult an expert whose job it is to keep track—your lawyer.

CONTENTS

INTRODUCTION

I received a phone call one morning from a man in Michigan who was supposed to come to New York to testify in a multimillion dollar lawsuit. He was calling a few days before he was scheduled to appear as a witness, to tell me that, due to an important business meeting, he would not arrive until a couple of hours before his deposition was scheduled to commence. That date and time for the deposition had been set by the court. I spent some time convincing him of the importance of the deposition and the need to be properly prepared, but he could not (or would not) change his plans.

I searched for some material to send, to help him prepare to testify. I asked a number of my colleagues if they had anything that would help. There was practically nothing available.

To make matters worse, his plane was late and he arrived less than half an hour before the deposition started. After doing my best, in a very short time, to prepare him for what was coming, I sat through a disastrous deposition session, feeling sorry about the way my witness was being taken advantage of, and wishing I could have done more to help him. What should have been a fairly routine case turned more complex with each mistake he made.

That was the last time I represented a witness who was ill suited to deal with the manipulations of the lawyers assigned to do the interrogation. I created a series of materials, and started giving them to my clients in advance to help assure their success at depositions.

This book will show you, with examples, the best way to prepare. It will take much of the mystery out of the legal process, and show you the most common errors that, depending on which side you're on, can make or ruin a case. You will find out how to avoid being tricked or trapped by experienced lawyers, and how to get your story out into the open so that it can be fairly judged.

The transcripts of testimony you will read are taken from actual depositions. The names, and some of the circumstances, have been changed to protect the identity of the litigants and lawyers involved.

HOW TO
Survive a
DEPOSITION

1

DISCOVERY

Chances are you're going to be sued. If not you, then at some point, the company you work for, the organization you help run, or a close family member or friend will be sued. Or else you'll sue somebody yourself or act as a witness in a case. No matter what your intentions, living in America means that the odds are you are likely to become involved with litigation.

In case you're not familiar with the term *litigation,* it refers to a legal proceeding, a lawsuit. In other words, a contest by judicial process. The number of legal contests started in this country each year continues to increase rapidly. The percentage of cases that proceed beyond the deposition stage, to a trial before a judge in a courtroom, is decreasing. However, the number of depositions used to dispose of lawsuits is increasing. The expanding use of depositions has greatly increased their importance.

It is estimated that in 1990, more than 17 million civil (noncriminal) lawsuits were pending in our state and federal courts. That boils down to about one lawsuit for every fifteen people. If you factor in the number of multiparty lawsuits, and the number of people who are called upon to testify in each case, it becomes clear that an awful lot of people are becoming involved in litigation.

Why are there so many lawsuits? One reason why we are currently seeing tremendous changes in the litigious nature of our society is that lawsuits encourage more lawsuits.

There are more lawyers in this country than ever before. About 30,000 new lawyers seek admission to the bar in the United States every year. To make a living, lawyers now resort to competing for clients.

Cases that would never have been encouraged in the past have become fodder for the increasingly hungry legal system. People who would never have thought of taking formal legal action in the past have more recently changed their outlook. The increasing number of lawsuits is leading to acceptance of litigation as a way of life. There were a lot fewer courts and judges 20 or 30 years ago.

So many lawsuits are currently being filed that in some areas of the country a new case may have to wait three or four years before the local court has time for a trial. Even though more than 90 percent of our civil lawsuits are settled or discontinued before trial, our legal system has come dangerously close to breaking down under its backlogged caseload. If it's not settled or dismissed before trial, a single case can tie up a courtroom for weeks, or even months.

DISPOSING OF CASES

Your deposition is part of a scheme that's supposed to help dispose of lawsuits and increase the efficiency of the court system.

There are only four potential solutions available to alleviate the overcrowding in our civil court system: 1. discourage litigation; 2. build more courts and hire more judges and court personnel; 3. dispose of cases before trial; 4. make trials move more efficiently through the courtroom.

The first two solutions have proven to be unworkable. In fact, the opposite seems to be happening. Instead of discouraging litigation our society finds more and more reasons to sue. Instead of increasing the number of courts that handle civil cases, our judicial system is often forced to bear the brunt of the government's budgetary wrangling. Federal, state, and local courts are often forced to cut back on personnel in order to deal with annual fiscal crises.

Only the last two solutions are really available to reach our constitutional objectives. To increase access to the courts, when a trial eventually starts, heightened efficiency is mandated to move the case through the system. But to deal fairly with each case, alternatives to a full trial have become necessary.

DISCOVERY SYSTEMS

In theory, most cases will be settled or compromised if the parties are able to prejudge the outcome for themselves. Litigants are naturally inclined to avoid the vexatious ordeal of a trial if they think they already know the most likely result. Knowing this, our lawmakers started looking for ways to ensure that each party has access to the information necessary to paint a clear picture of the battle that will be faced upon entering the courtroom. Laws were enacted to permit investigation through access to witnesses and evidence.

Clearly, permitting contestants to discover each others' evidence helps to avoid many contests. As a further benefit, contests that can't be totally avoided can at least be shortened by thorough preparation.

On television, legal cases always seem to hinge on the surprise witness, the just-discovered exhibit, or a theory that no one could have foreseen. In reality, this almost never happens under our present system. Major surprises are usually eliminated long before the case reaches the courtroom.

It's as if the courts now say to the litigants, "Find out everything you can about your opponent's strengths and weaknesses so that we can shorten the contest. Discover all you can about the evidence to be presented at trial. Discover what your opponent has to show the court and what the witnesses will say."

In fact, the system that has evolved to promote the adequate preparation and compromise of lawsuits is referred to as the *discovery* system. Almost every court has some sort of discovery system set up.

There are many ways to discover the evidence. Exchanging documents, identifying witnesses, obtaining reports and photographs, and answering written questions posed by the lawyers are a few of the ways that parties can gain access to evidence before the trial. This book concentrates on the method of gathering evidence that is considered by lawyers to be the most effective, efficient, and important of all available discovery procedures—the deposition.

After depositions, the potential outcome of the case may become clear, eliminating the need to continue the lawsuit.

2

EXAMINATION BEFORE TRIAL

We're all familiar with the examinations of witnesses that take place during a trial, commonly referred to as *direct* examination and *cross-examination*. Less familiar is the fact that most civil cases also involve one or two examinations that take place outside the courtroom in the form of depositions.

By simple definition, a civil deposition [also referred to as an *examination before trial* (EBT) or *examination under oath* (EUO)] is merely a question-and-answer session between witnesses (often parties to the lawsuit) and lawyers. On the surface, this sounds like a straightforward procedure, but in truth, a deposition is an expensive and ultimately important exercise, involving strategy, know-how, and often, ulterior motives. A deposition can turn a poor case into a gold mine, or completely foul up a good case if not properly handled. You and your lawyer both need extensive preparation to conduct a deposition successfully and to prevent the procedure from causing undue damage.

Seeing the legal system as it is usually portrayed in the media, one might get the impression that a lawsuit is started and a few minutes later (after one or two commercial breaks), everyone goes to court. Obviously, this isn't so.

The idea that everyone is entitled to his or her day in court is a common misconception. A case must meet certain threshold requirements before litigants are entitled to take up the court's time. These threshold requirements are often developed through the deposition process.

Take the deposition seriously. It may substitute for an in-court trial.

Unfortunately, because depositions are a "behind the scenes" part of the litigation, most people are not familiar with what is involved, and are dangerously unaware of the consequences of approaching the proceedings blindly. The cases that we hear about, or read about, are most often the ones that end up at trial. For every case that goes to trial, there are eight or nine that only go as far as having depositions. Sometimes the lawyers and litigants settle the case, and sometimes a judge reviews the deposition testimony and summarily decides or dismisses the case.

Since the case may be settled, dismissed, or otherwise concluded as a result of the testimony at the deposition, the examination before trial procedure may well be the climax of the case. In other words, **the deposition may, in effect, actually be the trial.** A deposition may be the only opportunity you have to present your evidence. The examination before trial may, in reality, turn out to be an examination *instead* of trial.

3

TEN REASONS FOR DEPOSITIONS

Why have depositions? They're expensive, time consuming, and often an unpleasant experience for the witnesses involved. Lately, they have also become so ingrained in the legal system that most lawyers consider a civil deposition to be a necessity rather than merely an option.

Proper preparation for your deposition requires that you be aware of the motives, intentions, and forces underlying the procedure. To understand what happens at an examination before trial, we begin by looking at the real reasons the lawyers want to conduct the proceeding.

REASON #1—ENGAGE IN DISCOVERY

The stated purpose for the deposition is, of course, for discovery. Another way to put it is "fishing around." A deposition provides the opportunity to find out if a provable case (or a provable defense) exists. It's an effective way to find out the witness' version of the alleged facts of the lawsuit by digging through the potential evidence to be presented orally at trial.

For example, in a lawsuit concerning a contract, one or more of the parties may allege that the written contract document did not contain the entire agreement. A deposition may be held to pin down exactly what each side will claim the agreement was supposed to be.

A deposition's primary purpose is discovery, but be aware of the nine other major reasons lawyers like to use them.

In the past, these fishing expeditions were frowned upon by the courts. Depositions were only taken when a witness was likely to be unavailable at the trial. Deposition testimony was not accepted in court if the witness could testify in person. Depositions were used only as a last resort.

Now that advance discovery of evidence is a highly touted principle of law, which has taken the place of the element of surprise during trial, the use of depositions has changed drastically. Through the increased practice of using depositions, lawyers have found many uses for the procedure in addition to mere discovery. There are at least nine other motives for conducting an examination before trial.

REASON #2—ASSESS THE WITNESS

The deposition is usually the first opportunity lawyers have to meet the witnesses for the opposition. It is also usually the first opportunity attorneys have to see how their own witnesses will do under fire.

At some point, or perhaps several times after the lawsuit is started, a lawyer and client will have to evaluate their position and make a decision about whether to take the case all the way. When deciding whether to proceed to trial, the lawyer must try to guess how the judge or jury will react to the case. One of the major factors to consider is the impression that each witness will make at trial.

Obviously, if your side has one or two good witnesses, and everyone on the other side appears to be a babbling idiot, you're not going to hesitate to take the case all the way. On the other hand, if your witnesses are weak, and the other side has witnesses that make a favorable impression, you will be less likely to push the case.

A deposition is used as a rehearsal to see the impression each witness will make if the case goes to trial.

What makes a good impression will vary from case to case. It may be desirable to have a witness who generates sympathy—for example, one who arrives in a wheelchair, or appears naive, or gives the impression of being sincere but simple-minded when you are up against a major corporation in a complicated matter. On the other hand, if the case will come down to an opinion-against-opinion battle of experts, the attorney will want the expert witness to appear experienced and knowledgeable beyond doubt.

Whatever the attorney is looking for, the first real feel for the possible presentation of the case comes when there is an opportunity to observe the witnesses at a deposition. The attorney may find that a witness whose testimony is significant is uncontrollable. There may also be certain aspects of a witness's conduct that can be corrected slightly, through coaching, to improve the impression at trial, or personal attributes of an opponent's witness that can be manipulated to provide an advantage. Once there has been an opportunity to watch the witnesses perform, the lawyer no longer has to guess about what will happen at trial. A good lawyer can evaluate the possible outcome of the contest by the potential impact each witness will have in court.

Lawyers don't usually remember every witness they see at every deposition, but they usually put some notes in the file regarding appearance, mannerisms, and other details about the individual. These notes can be reviewed months or years later when it is time to reevaluate the case. When the case is on the courthouse steps, and strategic decisions have to be made, the notes help to refresh memories of the overall impression made by a particular witness.

Recently, in reviewing some old files, I found notes I had made such as: "gets mixed up easily"; "makes faces"; "good on dates and details"; "evasive"; "extremely nervous"; "finger tapper"; "attended in soiled work clothes"; "wore leather jacket and hat in warm EBT room"; "squints before answering each question"; "well developed sense of humor"; "Tammy Bakker school of hair and makeup." In Chapters 14, 19, and 20, we will discuss in greater detail the tremendous effect manners and appearance often have on how successful or unsuccessful a witness may be.

REASON #3—PRESERVE TESTIMONY AND AUTHENTICATE EVIDENCE

One of the original reasons for inventing depositions was to preserve the testimony of a witness or to authenticate evidence. This is still a highly useful practice.

Occasionally, there is a witness who, for one reason or another, may not show up when the case is called for trial in two or three years. The witness may be ill, planning to leave the country, or too old to travel. Witnesses may move out of state, or may just refuse to cooperate. If the examination under oath is conducted properly, the testimony is a matter of record that can be presented to the court at the time of trial. In this way, the testimony can be used even if the witness is not present.

Sometimes the deposition testimony can be presented in court instead of a live witness.

It used to be that a witness had to be dead or in jail before deposition testimony could be used in court. The rules on admitting depositions into evidence have been relaxed considerably. Under the rules in many courts, the deposition transcript may now be presented at trial if the witness is more than 100 miles away, in prison, or otherwise unavailable. The term *unavailable* has been interpreted by various courts to mean everything from "the witness claims he can't be forced to testify because of special privilege," to "the witness refuses to testify despite a court order." Deposition transcripts have also been offered in evidence where a witness has claimed a memory loss about the subject upon which he previously testified.

Sometimes, due to the delay involved in getting cases to trial, a plaintiff (the one bringing the lawsuit) or a defendant may die before the case is heard. If there is a recorded deposition, where the opposing party has had the opportunity for cross-examination, it may still be possible to continue with the case and proceed to trial even though one of the parties is dead!

Making an adequate record becomes extremely important in these situations. By deposing witnesses, a lawyer can obtain important admissions on the record or preserve critical testimony for presentation at trial.

By the same token, if there is other evidence, in the form of records, documents, or photographs, that a witness could testify about, and if these items need to be presented in court for one party to be successful, they must be authenticated or the court will not consider them. Evidence that is authenticated at a deposition may be used at trial, even though the witness is not available to testify in person about its authenticity.

When you receive a notice that you are scheduled for a deposition, one of the first things to do is to start thinking about any items of evidence that you will need to have with you when you testify. Think about who has the evidence and where it may be located. If an item of evidence is in the possession of another party, your lawyer may take steps to have it produced at the scene of the deposition.

REASON #4—TEST THE WATER . . . FOR ALLIGATORS

More than evidence is revealed at a deposition. The examination before trial is an opportunity to observe strategy. The points upon which the opposing lawyer asks questions, and the aspects of the case that are examined in great detail, are key indicators of what the opposition has planned.

At the same time, the deposition session gives the lawyer a chance to test theories of the case by asking questions to seek out a reaction. By observing how the opposition responds and reacts, an experienced attorney can tell whether a particular area requires more in-depth investigation.

The deposition may be viewed as a testing ground for the eventual trial. The story each witness will tell will be sufficiently pinned down. Everyone involved in the lawsuit will be able to anticipate the most likely answers the witness will give to the questions that will be asked in front of the judge and jury.

There's an old saying that a good trial lawyer never asks a question during trial without already knowing what the answer will be. A trial is a well-planned presentation of evidence and not a time for experimentation. At a deposition, on the other hand, the lawyer has the chance to test the questions. The lawyer will use the deposition responses to hone the questioning so that at trial she solicits only the information she wants heard in the courtroom. By carefully choosing the way each question is eventually worded, the lawyer can effectively prevent a witness from spouting collateral information. Testing the questions at the deposition provides the lawyer with the opportunity to exercise control over the witness at trial.

Lawyers use depositions to test their strategy for presenting the case in the courtroom, and to try to determine the opposition's strategy.

Reason #5—Narrow the Issues

Although lawyers can clarify certain points through paperwork that goes back and forth between them, the deposition provides an ideal opportunity to determine the minute details upon which the parties disagree. Naturally, it follows that the parties will actually agree upon some points regarding factors relevant to the suit.

Finding out where the parties agree and disagree simplifies the job of proving the case at trial. Having prequestioned the opposition witnesses at the deposition, the attorney will know which areas need proving and which do not. To shorten the time needed to try the case, parties often agree to have certain issues or evidence admitted by stipulation (prior agreement) before the trial begins.

Depositions help shorten a trial by pinning down points on which everyone can agree.

REASON #6—LAY TRAPS FOR EFFECTIVE CROSS-EXAMINATION

If the witness makes a mistake during the deposition, the opposition's lawyer can take advantage and try to have the witness repeat the mistake at trial. This gives the opposition the chance to try to make the witness look foolish. It also provides a trap to discredit a witness who tries to change testimony at trial.

Mistakes can be used to discredit the witness during a trial.

A transcript of the deposition may be used at trial for the purposes of *impeachment*. This means that the witness is confronted with the inconsistent statements in order to challenge the validity of the testimony at trial. The opposing attorney can bring out the transcript in front of the judge and jury and force the witness to admit that he has changed his story. The lawyer can then attack the entire accuracy of the witness' memory or make it appear that the witness is purposely lying.

This is one of the most important uses for a deposition. Entire cases can change based on errors in deposition testimony. Witnesses whose stories appear to have changed at the time of trial lose the all-important element of believability.

REASON #7—HARASS THE OPPOSITION

Attorneys are officers of the court. They are supposed to use the legal system only to serve the ends of justice, and not for any ulterior motives. Unfortunately, in an effort to vigorously represent a client, an attorney may occasionally, unwittingly or otherwise, become involved in abusing the legal system. Because some lawyers unscrupulously play every angle to win, instead of trying to find the truth, depositions are sometimes used to worry or annoy the opposition.

Even the best attorneys sometimes hope that they can merely break the will of the opposition by putting a witness through the ringer. The legal system can be frustrating. It is also expensive. The more consuming the litigation becomes, the less likely that the litigants will be able to carry out their ultimate purpose.

Unscrupulous lawyers and litigants may try to use the deposition process as a means to annoy you.

People don't like to interrupt their daily lives to attend legal proceedings. Busy executives find it hard to take time to prepare and testify at a deposition. Individuals and companies who don't have adequate resources may decide that they don't want to invest in expensive litigation procedures. They may give up just because of the potential costs involved.

A deposition is often an uncomfortable procedure. A witness who is pressured at the examination before trial may not look forward to repeating the experience at an actual trial. It's an unfortunate fact of life in our legal system that justice sometimes suffers at the hands of litigants who use depositions to wear out the patience and resources of the opposition, or worse, merely to be vindictive.

Judges are not completely blind to these abusive practices. Some courts have begun to impose stiff penalties against parties and attorneys if an attempt is made to misuse the system for the purpose of harassment.

It would be wise to note that an attempt to use a deposition to harass an opponent can backfire. If you encourage your attorneys to proceed with a deposition, and it doesn't go as planned, it can ultimately bolster the confidence of the opposition.

Reason #8—Increase Fees

Expanding the legal proceedings increases the expense of the litigation and increases the amount of money lawyers can make from the system. Unless the case is being handled on a contingency basis, a lawyer will usually make more money if there is a series of depositions. Although multiple depositions can always be excused under the premise that thorough discovery is needed for adequate prosecution/defense of a lawsuit, some attorneys clearly are inclined to bill the client as much as they can.

An avaricious lawyer may see a deposition as merely another billing opportunity.

Reason #9—Encourage Settlement/ Dispose of the Case

Theoretically, any opportunity to evaluate the case and assess the potential outcome will help to encourage the parties to avoid a trial and resolve the case out of court. This is one of the most positive reasons for having depositions. When litigants are forced to listen to the opposition, they are more likely to treat the matter rationally, put aside personal feelings, and take a hard look at where the case is going.

A lawyer may plan to use the deposition to get the opposition to change its position and increase a prior settlement offer. She may also use the examination before trial to convince her own client of the true value of the case. Many times an adequate settlement offer is made, but the settlement is not accepted until one of the parties listens to the testimony. A deposition can be used to develop a sense of reality and delete the false hopes of one of the litigants.

It is human nature to fall into the "not my fault" syndrome. People convince themselves, or refuse to admit, that they are in any way responsible for anything negative that has happened. A rigorous afternoon of trying to answer pointed questions may cause such a person to reconsider a particular position.

Occasionally, litigants get as far as examination before trial and decide that they can't prove their case at all. They may also decide that the case is of such little value that it isn't worth further time or effort. The deposition experience may also prompt certain witnesses (especially independent volunteer witnesses who are not parties to the lawsuit) to develop a desire to excuse themselves from further participation.

Depositions may resolve the case because, once the testimony comes out, litigants may change their minds or a judge may conclude the case without a formal trial.

After the deposition, the court usually becomes directly involved in trying to resolve the case without a trial. The judge will often hold one or two pretrial settlement conferences. At these sessions, the lawyers appear and discuss their clients' positions with the judge and with opposing counsel. Their positions are usually based upon the results of the pretrial disclosure. It is not unusual, in attempting to settle, for an attorney to tell the judge exactly what was said at a deposition, or to show the judge a copy of the record of testimony.

The record of testimony may also be shown to the judge to dispose of the case as a matter of law. Sometimes the court will dismiss the case. The judge will review the facts and available evidence and determine that the law will not allow the case to proceed any further. The judge may also make a determination that one of the parties must win without a trial because the law says so under the circumstances.

Of course, the judge must have some sort of record of the facts so that there is something upon which to base the decision. A judge won't just take the attorney's word for it, and won't decide the case without a trial if there are important facts in doubt. However, a judge will usually take into account the sworn testimony of a deposition witness because it is assumed that the testimony would be the same if the witness were brought in to testify at trial.

REASON #10—IMPROVE THE CHANCES OF A JUST RESULT

Above all, an examination before trial is a chance to prepare for the trial that may follow. The more evenly prepared the litigants are, the more likely that justice will be done.

At the deposition, the parties try to discover and eliminate potential surprises. They then prepare for the manner in which they will use the evidence to their best advantage. They can save their and the court's time by getting ready to present the case in the best possible manner. For example, the time needed for trial may be reduced by presenting a few portions of the deposition testimony instead of calling the actual witness to testify in court.

An examination before trial helps lawyers get the case organized. It helps the parties avoid some of the confusion that might be present if the trial were started without prior discovery. In the long run, eliminating the confusion will help the judge and jury to determine the facts and law that are best applied to do justice under the circumstances.

Depositions help to get the case organized before it goes to court.

4

THE PLAYERS

There are three types of people involved in a deposition: attorneys, witnesses, and a stenographer commonly referred to as the *court reporter*. Each has a separate and important role to play in the proceeding. You should have a basic understanding of the function of each of these key people in order to gain insight into the strategy underlying the deposition.

THE ATTORNEY

Why does a litigant need an attorney? Some litigants do attempt to conduct their own cases. They are foolish. An untrained litigant who goes up against an experienced trial attorney is like a kid with a pen knife trying to fence with Zorro. This is true even at the beginning stages of litigation.

Although you only plan to attend the deposition and tell the truth, having a lawyer present to represent you will make things go smoother, take less time, and reduce the chances of your falling prey to the tricks of the opposing counsel who will be trying to twist your testimony into damaging evidence. It should also ease your completely understandable anxiety about this experience.

Law, like most professions, is becoming increasingly specialized. There are tax lawyers, general practitioners, matrimonial and family lawyers, criminal lawyers (referring to those who prosecute and defend criminal cases, not lawyers who are criminals), real estate lawyers, and patent and copyright lawyers, to name a few. Many states now have special education and experience requirements that attorneys must meet before they can claim to practice in a specialized area.

Many of the specialities overlap. For example, within each speciality there are lawyers who try cases and some who do not. We grow up thinking that all lawyers go to court and do trials, because that is what we see on TV. The fact is that over the years the percentage of lawyers who actually conduct trials has been declining. Many lawyers will now handle a case through the preliminary stages, and then refer the matter to a trial specialist later.

Don't be intimidated. Even attorneys, who are usually specialists at conducting depositions, make mistakes.

At the deposition, you will usually find a separate attorney representing each of the parties to the lawsuit. No matter what the training and qualifications of each lawyer, they all have one thing in common. They are all human and subject to the same human faults, virtues, and weaknesses we all have. It is important to keep this in mind for two reasons. First, it helps to keep you from being intimidated by the opposing lawyer. Second, you can't expect perfection from your own lawyer.

A litigation specialist can receive all the training and experience necessary to effectively conduct a case, but will still make mistakes occasionally. Trial lawyers are not as godlike as some may wish or pretend them to be. They are, however, molded under intense pressure. Good trial lawyers are on the firing line almost every day. They are almost constantly subjected to the scrutiny of the courts and other members of the bar.

There are abundant anecdotes about stupid questions that highly trained lawyers have asked during trials and at depositions:

> "You say you've never seen this contract before, but my question is do you remember signing it?"
> "When you were lying there in this unconscious state, did you see him coming or try to get out of the way?"
> "Was the tree in the middle of the road or on the side?"
> "You were alone in the car. Okay, were you the driver?"
> "If the rental was for $5,000 for the first six months, for how long of a period would it have been at $16,000? True or false?"
> "You recall performing the autopsy at approximately 8:35 P.M.? And was Mr. Smith dead at that time?"
> "Now, Mrs. Jones, you claim to have given birth to your first child in April 1980, and you gave birth to a total of three

children during the course of your marriage, and you claim
that each of these children was yours, is that correct?"
"Is that the same nose you broke when you were a child?"
"Where did you live for the one-year period before you were
born?"

All those questions were asked by highly educated lawyers who
were consumed by their effort to make a case for their clients.

Even if you have the luxury to choose the lawyer/litigation specialist who will personally represent you at the EBT, the best you can
do is help prepare thoroughly and hope the attorney will be effective.
Lawyers often carry malpractice insurance because the legal system has
become so complex that even specialists can't possibly know it all.

On the other hand, you certainly have the right to expect that the
attorney will use all appropriate effort to competently and vigorously
represent you.

THE REPORTER

Reporters, sometimes referred to as *court reporters* even though they
may not be connected with the actual court, are highly skilled and
trained stenographers.

Some still use the shorthand style of reporting. They flip through
the pages of a stenographic notebook making shorthand squiggles.
More commonly, modern reporters use shorthand machines, which
resemble dwarf typewriters.

The newer machines are compatible with computer wordprocess-
ing equipment to make the reporter's task easier. Shorthand notes are
recorded on a computer tape or disc and printed out in full by a computer printer. The machines that make the computer tape recordings
also make a paper copy of the shorthand notes in case the tape is accidentally erased.

The reporter's job is to take down everything that is said by the witnesses and the attorneys. The reporter's notes are then made into a
typed transcript of the complete testimony.

The reporter is also usually qualified as a notary public, and is
often the one who administers the oath and swears in the witness who
will testify.

The reporter usually keeps the stenographic notes on hand for several years following the deposition. If a dispute arises about what was actually said during the deposition, the reporter may be called into court to testify by reading from the actual shorthand notes.

Litigants often ask why the courts haven't resorted to tape recording or some other manner of making a record of the testimony. True, some depositions are videotaped for presentation at trial, but, even where a video recorder is in operation, most jurisdictions still require a court reporter to take down what is said.

Perhaps the rationale is that electronic recordings are unreliable because they can be tampered with. There is also the danger of erasure. Courts have determined that the one way to ensure that a recording is reliable is to have a court reporter present who can verify what was said. Recording the proceeding by other than stenographic means is rare because, since the reporter has to be present anyway, it seems unnecessary in most situations to bother making a separate recording.

Whatever the reason, court reporters are very much a part of the system. Indeed, a court reporter is a marvel to observe. Most reporters can write at a rate of between 200 and 300 words per minute. It is truly amazing to see how they manage to keep up with what is being said, even during a heated debate between witnesses and counsel.

Of course, the reporter has to be completely unbiased. The stenographer is a neutral party who is supposed to take down everything that is said, word-for-word and sound-for-sound.

The stenographer takes down everything that is said during the deposition, word-for-word, and produces a written transcript of the proceedings.

According to the National Shorthand Reporters Association Handbook, the reporter is permitted to do a certain amount of judicious editing, without changing the sense of what was said, to correct unintentional language faults of the attorneys. However, the sworn testimony of witnesses must be reproduced exactly as given.

Stenographers often spell unfamiliar words phonetically and then, after the deposition, look them up to fill them in correctly. In that way, they do not have to interrupt the proceeding to ask for the correct spelling of a word. Usually, the reporter will also ask for the spelling of unfamiliar names at the beginning or end of the deposition.

In most areas of the country, the reporter is paid an appearance fee and is then paid by the page for producing copies of the transcript of testimony. The party who requested the deposition usually pays for the services of the reporter, although, in multiparty litigation, the reporter's fees are often shared.

WITNESSES

Anyone who has information bearing upon the issues involved in a lawsuit is a potential witness. Anyone who has information that may lead to other relevant information also is a potential witness.

There are three basic categories of witnesses who appear in a lawsuit: parties, independents, and experts.

The most common deposition witness is a party to the litigation. This category also includes representatives of a party, such as an officer of a corporation, or an employee of a business.

The independent, or nonparty witness, is usually someone who personally has nothing to do with the lawsuit, but may have some information that is relevant to it. A bystander who witnessed an accident is a good example of someone who may be called to testify as a nonparty witness.

While a litigant usually has a right to depose any other party in the lawsuit, different rules apply to taking a deposition of a nonparty witness. Often an attorney must obtain permission from the court before the nonparty may be deposed. Attorneys usually try to obtain the testimony of an independent witness by means of cooperation, however, if the witness will not cooperate, the attorney may go to court and get an order from the judge to compel the independent witness to testify.

The other type of witness, the so-called expert, is sometimes referred to as a "hired gun." This is a witness who is employed, and usually well paid by one of the parties, for the specific purpose of giving evidence. There are some people who make their living as experts, hiring themselves out to go from trial to trial giving testimony on specific areas of expertise. Since just about everyone is qualified to be an expert on some subject, the topic of expert testimony will be dealt with in greater detail in Chapter 7.

Anyone who has relevant information may be a witness, but different rules apply for getting different types of witnesses to testify.

5

MORAL SUPPORTERS

"Tis not enough to help the feeble up, but to
support him after."

Shakespeare, Timon of Athens I.i

Having described the players who are necessary to a deposition, it is
important at this point to mention another individual or group who
is often unnecessary, and sometimes detrimental. It is not unusual to
have friends, relatives, co-workers, or other moral supporters show up
at the deposition with the witness. Depending upon the circumstances,
this can be a good practice or a very bad idea.

In the past, I have seen situations where big brothers showed up to
lend support to their siblings, parents have arrived to support their children (and "children" to support their elderly parents), and bosses to
lend support to their employees.

If the deposition room is large enough, the witness may request
that these extra people sit in during the testimony. If the extra person is
not an independent witness who will be called upon to testify, the attorneys will usually consent to the moral supporter sitting in the room. It
may be helpful for the witness to have a friendly and familiar face in the
room while testifying. As the following examples point out, however,
the presence of a nonwitness can have dire consequences.

DRAWBACKS

I recall a case involving several teenagers, where all except one showed
up with their parents. It was a case with plenty of insurance coverage,

which could easily have been settled if the witnesses had been willing to tell the truth. The situation involved a young girl and her boyfriend who were engaged in some sex-play in the back seat of a moving automobile when a traffic accident took place causing the girl to be injured.

Listening to the testimony of the kids whose parents were present, you would have thought that everyone in the car had been sitting up straight, with their seatbelts fastened, in complete silence, with the radio off, carefully watching the road and concentrating on assisting the driver (except for the occasional pause to help straighten each other's halos). However, when the one young man who attended the examination without his parents testified, what really had been going on in the car became obvious. Unfortunately, by the time the young man gave the uninhibited testimony, the other witnesses were already on record and were stuck with the fables they had concocted.

It's hard to blame them, since it was obviously an embarrassing situation for all who were involved. They merely couched their stories in a manner they thought would be acceptable in front of their parents. If only they had realized how much better off they would have been in the long run by having the truth come out at the deposition, they could each have saved thousands of dollars in litigation expenses. The conflicting testimony caused an otherwise settleable case to go to a full jury trial. Needless to say, the halos fell off rather dramatically in the courtroom, despite the presence of the parents at trial.

Beware of inviting people to sit in for their moral support—their mere presence may be turned against you.

Even though the moral supporter may have nothing to say, and may sit quietly in a corner throughout the examination, sharp opposition attorneys may try to use the presence of the nonwitness to their client's advantage. The attorney may ask the court reporter to note on the record that the nonwitness is in the room. If the nonwitness leaves the room at any point and returns, these facts may also be noted on the record. This information may later be used quite deviously by the opposing side.

For example, if the witness tries to claim at the trial that he made a mistake during the deposition because he was nervous, the attorney might use the presence of the nonwitness to try to show that the environment at the deposition was tolerable. The attorney can do this by noting that the record indicates the witness had a spouse or a friend in the deposition room to lend moral support.

Lawyers also find it handy to note the presence of the other people in the room in case one of them is called as a witness at the trial. Friends, relatives, or co-workers often have information that, as the case proceeds, makes them likely witnesses. If their presence was noted on the record during previous testimony, it is easy for one of the attorneys to say something like, "You were present when so-and-so testified, and you've already heard their version of the story. . . ." This can cast serious doubts on the veracity and independence of their future testimony.

Another variety of common moral supporter who often shows up at a deposition in a corporate lawsuit is the boss or supervisor. Usually this person arrives to "help" a company employee testify about the company business. For some reason, companies often feel compelled to send along one or two superiors, and sometimes a separate company lawyer, when an employee is selected to be a witness.

In one case I recall, the security guard for a particular company did a good job of testifying and supported his company's position, much to the satisfaction of the defense lawyer and the company personnel manager who attended for moral support. The witness had no reason to lie, and the company had nothing to hide. The witness had been with the company for five years, and his employer had quite obviously given some thought to the prospect that this employee would be the best and most knowledgeable witness to testify. The company chose the witness because they thought he would make a good impression, and they were right—at first.

Unfortunately, as is the American way, this particular employee did not stay with the company forever. In fact, he sought and obtained another job, at higher pay, about eight months after the deposition. When the case finally came up for trial, it was almost two years after his examination under oath, and the witness was subpoenaed to come and testify even though he no longer worked for the company being sued.

Prior to taking the stand, the witness was well prepared by the defense attorneys. His testimony mostly went over the same ground that he had covered at the deposition. On one minor point, however, he suffered a slight memory lapse and testified incorrectly.

The point on which he made a mistake really wasn't very important to the case. It became important, however, in the light of considering the witness's credibility. The opposing attorney seized upon the mistake and the circumstances of the previous deposition as follows:

Q. But that's not what you previously testified to, is it?
A. Well, it is and, I'm not really sure now, but—
Q. You just read the transcript I gave you of your prior testimony?
A. Yes.

Q. And what you're telling us now is different from the—

A. I'm not saying it's different, just that I can't recall.

Q. Sir, when you testified at the deposition, you were still an employee of the XYZ corporation, weren't you?

A. Yes.

Q. And in fact, when you testified at the deposition, Mr. Dithers was present in the room during the examination before trial, was he not?

A. I don't,—I,—yes.

Q. Mr. Dithers was the company personnel manager, right?

A. He was at the time, I'm not sure what he—

Q. He was the person in charge of hiring and firing for the company, was he not?

A. Yes, I think so.

Q. And he was there in the room when you testified in May 1989?

A. Yes.

Q. And now that you're not testifying with your boss in the room, your testimony seems to be changing. Well, I have no further questions for you.

The impression that the attorney was trying to leave in the minds of the jurors is obvious. Without coming right out and saying it, the attorney was accusing the witness of having lied to please his boss. If the jury accepted the hint, the entire testimony of this witness would be damaged. Credibility plays an important role in the minds of jurors who are trying to assess the conflicting tales told by witnesses at trial. If jurors think that a witness was under pressure to testify differently because a boss was in the room, they might discount the witness's entire story as being given under some measure of duress.

Another danger is that the bystander may be tempted to physically react, accidentally providing a clue that will alert the opposition. Facial expressions and body language can tip off the opposition to the existence of undisclosed information.

THE OCCASIONAL ADVANTAGES

This is not to say that a company should never send another representative to the deposition, or that a friend or relative should never accompany the deponent for moral support. On several occasions, I have found nonwitnesses to be helpful during preparation sessions. I recall one occasion when certain documents from a company file contained apparently conflicting dates. Luckily, while we were preparing for the testimony, a company vice president, who happened to accompany the witness, was able to get on the phone and obtain a quick explanation, saving the deponent from an embarrassing situation. However, instances where a moral supporter can prove useful are rare.

The occasional advantages to having moral supporters in attendance may not be worth the risk.

CONSIDER THE IMPRESSION

It is important to consider the impression the presence of the nonwitness makes. If you remember that one of the purposes of the deposition is to gauge the potential impact a particular witness will have if the case goes to trial, then, clearly, witnesses who are able to stand on their own two feet and testify will make a better impression than witnesses who need someone to hold their hand.

Another consideration is the temptation the witness may feel to refer to other people in the room when stuck on a question. If the witness starts looking to another person for answers, or reacts to the facial expressions of a friend in the room, or even just glances over before answering, the witness may make a poor impression in the eyes of the opposition.

You will generally make a better impression without moral supporters in the room.

On the other hand, witnesses who refer to nobody, and who make frequent eye contact with the attorney asking the questions, come across as knowledgeable and secure, and leave the impression that they will be believed in court, whether they have all the answers or not. Removing the moral supporters from the room also removes the temptation to look at them before answering.

THE DANGER OF WAIVING PRIVILEGED COMMUNICATIONS

Finally, there is the danger that the bystander may inadvertently become a witness after the fact. Conversations between an attorney and client are generally immune from discovery, with one important catch.

The immunity can be waived if someone else is present and overhears the conversation.

Keep communications with your attorney private as much as possible.

Bringing a moral supporter with you to a preparation session, or to any private meeting with your legal counsel, creates the danger that the bystander may later be called upon to talk about what was heard. Any conversation you have with a nonparty, other than your spouse or attorney, can become the subject of discovery. In other words, the independent party may be questioned about your conversation, and you may have accidentally waived your privacy.

If a neighbor drives you to the EBT, and then sits in the room during the testimony, you can be sure that the opposition is taking into account the likelihood that there has been some discussion between the two of you concerning the lawsuit. Won't the neighbor be surprised on being subpoenaed to testify about your conversation?

On the other hand, in some circumstances, the presence of a non-witness is very useful. The independent may pick up on things that the attorney missed while concentrating on the testimony, and may come away from the EBT session with a different impression regarding important aspects of the case. Some attorneys actually provide their own non-witnesses, in the form of associates or paralegals, who sit in the examination room to obtain an unbiased impression of the proceedings. It's best to consult your attorney before planning to have any nonwitness attend the deposition, and always best to exclude unnecessary people from your private conversations about the case.

6

THE COMPANY WITNESS

If you are the plaintiff or defendant, you probably have no choice but to testify. You can't pick someone else to take your place at the deposition. The rules are a little different, however, if one of the parties to the lawsuit is a business organization.

A company cannot speak for itself, so some qualified person has to show up and talk. In this situation, the attorney who wants to schedule the deposition may not know who in the organization has the requisite knowledge to testify. If the party is a giant corporation, the opposing lawyer obviously can't take the deposition of everyone in the company. Time would not allow this, and neither would the court.

CHOOSING THE COMPANY WITNESS

Because the court won't permit the entire business of the company to grind to a halt while every employee is brought in to testify, the burden of selecting the appropriate witness is usually shifted, in the first instance, to someone at the company. Instead of naming names, the deposition notice will name general subjects upon which the chosen witness must be prepared to provide information or a class of people expected to have such information. Someone at the company then has to pick the witness. Companies must consider a number of factors before making this important choice.

First, attorneys who try cases against large corporations love to try to depersonalize the organization in the eyes of the jury. They like to

If the opposition can't identify a particular witness, they can describe the subjects to be covered, and the company will have to select the appropriate witness.

play up the David and Goliath scenario. They try to show that the big, bad, impersonal, megabusiness entity is an unthinking and unfeeling creature, as opposed to the other parties in the courtroom who may be smaller, family-run businesses, or mere individuals.

This can have two effects on the case. First, it may make a company witness who speaks on behalf of the giant entity seem less believable. Second, it creates sympathy for the little guy. If it's a toss-up, and the jury has to hurt somebody, they usually feel less constrained to decide against the bigger, more intangible company, because they envision the smaller entity on a more personal level. To combat this, companies should try to pick what lawyers call "boy scout witnesses."

A company must give special consideration to the effect a witness can have in portraying it as a thinking, feeling group of people. Consideration must be given to how the appearance of the witness will be superimposed upon the company as a whole. The company's best choice will be an individual who is attractive, able to smile under pressure, and generally well spoken.

The lawyers in the deposition room know that, if the case ever gets to court, the jury will be looking at the company witness as representing the kind of people the company hires. Every person at the home office may be a rotten, conniving sleaze, but if the jury only sees Mother Theresa giving testimony, the inference will naturally be that everyone at the company is likely to be similar.

When there's a choice then, the thought given to choosing the witness should not be to convey "this is our employee," so much as to convey "this is the type of employee," or "this is the kind of people who make up our company behind the scenes." Generally, the larger the company, the more witnesses to choose from, and the greater the possibility of finding someone who oozes charm and credibility.

THE KNOW-NOTHING WITNESS

Attorneys utilize all kinds of ploys in plotting the strategy of a particular lawsuit. In the past, one of the favorite tactics has been to try to hide information by producing a deposition witness, or a series of witnesses, who have no knowledge of the subject matter.

The theory is that the opposition can be broken down over time by forcing a series of depositions to occur before allowing the examination of the individual who can actually answer the questions. This is a very dangerous tactic, which can have major consequences to the company if it backfires.

The company is obligated under the law to produce a spokesperson who can give the necessary information to complete discovery. The court will not look lightly upon a company that knowingly refuses to give up the information by playing dumb through its chosen witnesses. You can be sure that if the witness shows up and answers continually by saying, "I don't know that, you have to ask someone else at the company," the transcript of the testimony will wind up in front of a judge who will consider whether the company should pay a fine for obstructing the discovery process. Because the courts have increased the frequency of fines and sanctions for obstructive tactics, know-nothing witnesses have begun to disappear.

The company must produce a witness who is properly prepared to answer questions, and may be sanctioned by the court for failing to do so.

CONSENT

A corporation can request that you, as an employee, submit to a deposition and speak on behalf of the company, but if you are asked, you can decide to consent to testify or not. As a general rule, the company cannot force you to be a representative at a deposition without an order from the court. Usually, if there are other witnesses available, an attorney will advise the company not to produce an unwilling deponent.

Attorneys know that people react differently when they're unwillingly placed in an uncomfortable position. You may lose some of your charm if it's clear you don't want to be there. There is also the danger that an unhappy employee may do something, consciously or subconsciously, to sink the company in the litigation. So generally, you won't be forced to go if you don't want to.

Of course, there are times when a particular person is the only appropriate witness, and under these circumstances, you probably won't be able to avoid the deposition. If your individual testimony is crucial, and you are unwilling to participate, the court will grant an order compelling you to cooperate. In these circumstances, the opposition usually knows who they want to talk to, and they won't settle for anything less than the deposition of the target individual.

Unwilling employees are not usually forced to represent the company if alternative witnesses are available.

TARGETING TOP EXECUTIVES

Often, the top executives of the company will be specifically named by the opposition as the required witnesses for the deposition. There are three reasons for targeting top executives to appear.

First, the testimony of a top executive is given more weight. The judge and jury will not only consider what was said, but who had the authority to say it. In addition, it is unlikely that someone else from the company will come forward at a later date and try to contradict what the boss said under oath.

A deposition witness gives statements that bind the company. Everyone knows that different people within a corporate framework have different responsibilities and different levels of authority. The exception, of course, is the top executive who generally has authority over everything. The opposition knows that if they nail down the boss, they've nailed down everyone beneath the boss as well.

High ranking company executives are often targeted as witnesses by the opposition who hopes that they won't have the time to properly prepare or will settle the case to avoid testifying.

Second, top executives are less likely to spend the time necessary to properly prepare for the deposition. There's an assumption that the higher the executive is in the organization, the busier the person's lifestyle will be, and the less time the person will have to devote to the litigation.

There is also the likelihood that the executive will consider the matter being litigated trivial and not worth valuable time in the grand scheme of running the company. This, too, often leads to a lack of preparation, which the opposition can work to its advantage.

The third reason for targeting top executives is that, in the chain of responsibility, the top executive may bear some of the blame for whatever led to the lawsuit. This may cause the executive to have second thoughts about giving testimony, and may cause the executive to try to find a way to avoid the deposition altogether—such as quickly settling the case.

The company may also settle a poor case for a small amount (what is referred to in legal circles as *nuisance value*) if it decides that the top executive's time is worth more than bothering with the examination.

If the targeted executive doesn't want to testify, and if it can be shown to the court that there are other, more appropriate company witnesses, the company attorney may be able to apply to the court, sufficiently in advance of the scheduled deposition date, to have the judge determine whether it is truly necessary for the targeted witness to be the one who shows up.

PREPARING TO BE THE COMPANY WITNESS

It is not good enough for a witness who represents an organization, such as an officer or employee of a corporation, to appear and refuse to answer questions on the grounds of having no personal knowledge about the matter in question. The company has the duty to educate the employee about those matters.

When the company presents a proper witness, it will produce someone who can testify from personal knowledge where appropriate, and otherwise speak on behalf of the organization concerning information that is reasonably available. In other words, if one doesn't already exist, the company has the obligation to create a witness to answer the anticipated questions.

Of course, if you do not have all the required information at the deposition, it is likely that you will be asked to identify the person or persons who would know the answers. The attorneys may then proceed with further depositions of the additional company personnel (although sometimes a court order must first be obtained to permit further depositions).

Unfortunately, companies are sometimes too wary of lawyers who are involved with activities that cause employees to miss time from work. Corporate managers either don't understand or are unwilling to recognize the need to attend depositions. They are not always willing to cooperate without a mandate from the court compelling them to do so.

Attorneys who represent large corporations are often frustrated when they try to get the company to identify the best possible witness. The attorney's time and the corporation's assets are then wasted. Most companies do not have a system set up to deal with such situations.

Some of the more progressive companies recognize that doing business in the present environment will require company witnesses to give testimony with increasing frequency. These organizations have established witness training programs, to create readily available "boy scout" witnesses with information networks and investigatory systems that can deal with the various circumstances of litigation that regularly arise. The potential witnesses work with company lawyers to practice researching company records, and then conduct regular drills to cultivate skills in delivering effective testimony.

Unfortunately, most companies haven't yet caught on to the importance of being prepared in advance for litigation. They wait until the

Some companies have established witness training programs to prepare potential witnesses for litigation.

deposition notice has arrived, or until the examination is only a week or so away, before starting to select the individual who will, in effect, have to "become" the company for the purpose of testifying. Although you may have to endure a similar situation, and may have only a short time to prepare to adequately represent the company, there are some steps you can take to catch up.

"BECOMING" THE COMPANY

The company might have chosen you to be the deponent because they believe that you also will be a good witness if the case eventually proceeds to trial. They will expect that you not only know or can learn the required information, but also that you can deliver it in a manner that will make a good impression in the courtroom.

You will want to find out, as much as possible, the kinds of questions you will be asked and the subjects that will be covered. This may mean an extra preparation session with the attorney, because you will want the opportunity to research the necessary information in the company records, and to talk to other individuals at the company who can give direction and provide details.

As the company's chosen witness, you will be expected to know the corporate structure, work flow, and management systems.

You will have to become as familiar as possible with the inner workings of the company. You may also want to seek out people who have previously testified on the company's behalf (such as the person who held your job before being promoted) to discuss their experiences at prior depositions.

No matter how well prepared you are, there will be some questions that you can't answer, even though the information is available. In these situations, you will have to be familiar enough with the company job stratification to testify about who might have the information if you don't.

YOUR JOB TITLE

To have credibility at the first instance, if you are not one of the top executives, you may have to begin your preparation by adjusting your job title. Some companies bestow a brand new title on their witness, just for the purpose of sounding good at the deposition (and possibly later in the courtroom). If an adjustment is necessary, you may just add some words to your title that indicate your authority to speak about the subject at hand. Discuss this well in advance with your superiors and with the company lawyer.

For example, one organization I know recently sent a secretary from the personnel department to a deposition in an employment discrimination case. She was the person in charge of the complaint records and the process for handling investigations and responses. She was going to testify about the manner in which the company generally handled complaints of sexual harassment. Her title before the deposition was Administrative Assistant—Human Resources. When she arrived at the deposition, she was the Chief Human Resources Grievance Coordinator and Administrative Assistant. She was, of course, asked how long she had held that position, and she was able to testify that she had "generally had the same job duties for the last three years."

In other situations, the company will establish a special job position and a new title with special duties just to help with the case. For example, an auditor position may be created so that the company will have a witness who can review and analyze data specifically necessary to win the case.

It may be appropriate to refine your job title.

YOUR JOB DESCRIPTION

As a company witness, you will be asked some questions about your job duties, training, and experience. This will be necessary to convince the attorneys that you are qualified to testify, and in case you are no longer available, to convince the court that your testimony has some basis to be read into evidence if the case goes to trial.

Do not wait until you reach the deposition room to think about what you should say regarding your job. It may be too late to put all the relevant details together, and you may leave out something that would assure your qualifications.

Take a few minutes to jot down some notes about your job. Give the notes to your attorney to review at the preparation session. The following outline will help you to think about what to say, and will also help your attorney to ask the right questions when qualifying you to testify before the court:

Give advance thought to how you will testify about your job duties and experience.

1. My job title is—
2. My general job duties are—
3. My experience with the company includes—
   a. Number of years with the company—
   b. Time in my present position—
   c. Previous positions held with this company—
      i.   Time in each position—
      ii. Duties—
4. Previous similar work experience with other companies—
5. Background education—
   a. Undergraduate—
   b. Post-graduate—
   c. On-the-job-training—
   d. Special training or courses that may concern the issues in the case—
6. Relevant memberships and organizations—
7. Special relevant industry achievements, if any—

MAKING THE RIGHT IMPRESSION

The company witness generally maintains a different status from a witness who is personally involved in the litigation. The company witness has the advantage of not being automatically self-interested. This will lend an air of believability to your testimony, provided that you don't blow it by seeming to be the type of individual who will do or say anything the company wants.

One way to avoid looking too much like you're under the complete control of the company is to achieve the right physical appearance. You may want to avoid wearing your uniform, the company tie, or other attire (including hats, watches, rings, pens, etc.) bearing the company logo. It may be best to avoid bringing with you items such as briefcases, note pads, and portfolios emblazoned with the company emblem. You may even want to avoid arriving at the deposition (or at court) in a company vehicle. Other tips on how to dress to impress will be found in Chapter 14.

While you want to represent the company, you want to do so in a way that will show you are your own person, capable of using your own judgment, and a part of a company of people who, similarly, are not automatons acting at the will of the corporation. This attitude should be reflected in your testimony, by personalizing the company whenever possible, and avoiding answers phrased so that it might appear you are laying blame on the company.

When asked to testify about company policies or procedures, you might want to try using "we" and "our" to refer to the company, instead of speaking in terms like "the" or "their." It sounds much more personal to talk about "our" Quality Control Department than it does to speak in terms of "the quality control people." Similarly, it might be better to say "we, at the XYZ corporation, have set up a procedure," than to say "the company has set up a procedure," or worse yet, "they have a procedure." Even top executives, who make the ultimate decisions, may want to try personalizing the company through their testimony. Of course, this strategy should also be discussed with the attorney representing the company, because there are times when the purpose of your testimony would indicate a more direct approach, and you need to be mindful of avoiding the opposite extreme of sounding ridiculous (e.g., when you were in the control room alone but you testify that "we" were operating the machinery).

Personalize the company when giving appropriate testimony—use words such as "we" and "our."

7

ARE YOU AN EXPERT?

In one respect, everyone is an expert. We're all experts on different subjects at different times. But if you are a witness chosen for the deposition, it is usually because you are one of the only people, or perhaps the only person on earth, who has the knowledge or information required to aid the judge and jury in determining a particular issue.

Experts come in all forms, and from all walks of life. They can be medical experts, economists, engineers, or people with special knowledge gained during everyday activities.

For example, in a negligence case our office tried a few years ago, there was a question as to whether a parking lot at a major shopping center had been properly maintained. An employee testified that the parking lot was completely cleaned with a sweeping machine every morning. An "expert" was then brought in to contradict the employee's testimony. The expert was simply a fellow who drove a city street sweeper for a living.

Many kinds of experts are involved in litigation and a special diploma may not be necessary.

The street sweeper operator came in and testified about how long he thought it would take to clean the parking lot with a sweeping machine. In his expert opinion, it would have taken an entire day to go over the particular parking lot with a sweeping machine. His expertise came from his familiarity with operating similar machines as part of his daily job.

This man came under the category of a *skilled witness*, or a *lay expert*. Although he did not have formal education in the subject matter of his testimony, he had experience that gave him specialized knowledge and qualified him to give testimony.

While it is the usual practice to have depositions of the litigants in preparation for trial, and while independent witnesses are often deposed, it is less likely that pretrial testimony will be taken from an expert. Unless there is a compelling reason for the expert's deposition, this testimony is often saved for trial.

WHY EXPERTS ARE DEPOSED

Experts are usually deposed to preserve their testimony for trial, but also may be deposed for tactical reasons.

There are, however, certain circumstances under which experts are deposed. Sometimes depositions are used to determine the basis of the expert's opinion. This usually arises in cases where the litigation will boil down to a word-against-word battle of expert opinions. Instead of waiting until trial to hear what the opponent's expert has to say, a party will serve notice to take a deposition.

More often, experts are deposed because they will be unavailable for trial, and one of the parties wants to use the deposition testimony as evidence. In this situation, a party may take the deposition of its own expert.

For example, a plaintiff may serve notice to take the deposition of his treating physician if the doctor cannot be present for the trial. An engineer or laboratory investigator from another state, who may be unable to travel, or any of the myriad experts on various subjects who are located in different parts of the country, are likely to find themselves giving deposition testimony.

Sometimes taking an expert's deposition is purely a tactic to get the suit resolved. If there is a solid case and a highly qualified and unimpeachable expert to testify, taking a deposition may put the fear of God into the opposition. The record of the expert's testimony, if uncontradicted, might also help the judge to summarily decide the case without trial.

There is one other tactical reason to conduct an examination before trial of an expert. A deposition provides a good opportunity to see how an expert will hold up under fire.

BECOMING AN EXPERT WITNESS

Lawyers obtain the services of potential experts in many ways. Sometimes the experts are people who already have some familiarity with the subject matter of the case, such as a consulting designer or an accountant who previously had some input. Also, several organizations keep lists of experts in various fields. These include associations of trial attorneys, various bar associations, and private expert-finding services, known as expert banks, that sell information. These referral organizations keep track of expert witnesses, the kinds of cases they have been involved in, and the results they have obtained.

Some professional witnesses take out ads in publications such as legal journals or other publications likely to be seen by attorneys. Because experts often receive large hourly fees for their services, an expert who has a reputation for being experienced, qualified, and available has the potential for a considerable income. Hired gun witnesses command thousands of dollars for work as consultants in preparing the litigation and thousands more for attending and testifying at a trial or deposition. Depending on the type of expert, two or three hundred dollars an hour, or more, may be a reasonable fee for testifying.

In return for these megafees, litigants want experts who not only have the requisite knowledge, but who also have some other important qualifications. The cost of hiring the expert is balanced against the expert's potential ability to make whatever impression will be required to win the case.

Just about anyone can become an expert witness and command high fees for giving testimony.

A long list of credentials may be helpful, since these will be recited as part of the record, to let the judge and jury know that the expert is qualified to testify on the subject. (However, as in the case of the street sweeper, no specific academic credentials are required for someone to be an expert witness.)

Two other qualifications that are often considered are whether the expert is someone who has written on a particular subject or someone who has received awards or other recognition. A lawyer may try to track down someone who has published a particular article that is accepted as gospel by other experts in the same field. It is then possible to force the opposition's expert to admit under oath that the published expert is considered to be the authority.

Similarly, an expert who is somehow certified or a member of some professional organization, or has received awards or other recognition, is more likely to be influential at trial or during discovery. Judges, juries, and parties to the lawsuit will give greater consideration to what such an expert has to say.

The best expert witnesses usually become well known to members of the legal profession. If they do well assisting one litigator, they are likely to get repeat business or referrals. However, attorneys often have to rely on the services of an expert who is a total stranger.

It is dangerous to march into court with an expert witness who is an unknown quantity when the case hinges on that testimony. That is why some attorneys may prefer to have you testify at an EBT, and then make a decision about whether to use your services after seeing what you can do.

DRAWBACKS

Of course, there is a certain amount of danger in taking advance testimony from an expert. If the expert makes a mistake, the opposition might make the expert their own witness and use the expert against the party that originally retained the expert. By the same token, taking the deposition of an opposition expert may be a good tactic if you suspect that the opposition is bluffing.

There is also a danger in using an expert who testifies too often, if any prior testimony can be construed to be contradictory. Transcripts of prior depositions and courtroom testimony may be obtained for use as a tool to attack the expert's credibility. Anyone who wants to be a professional expert witness must be careful to be consistent and maintain veracity when subjected to an examination under oath.

A long list of credentials doesn't mean the testimony will be useful unless the expert knows how to get a point across.

Finally, take note that the most qualified expert doesn't always make the best impression. Experts can have outstanding credentials on an academic level and not make a good impression on a practical level. Someone speaking from actual experience usually sounds better than someone who testifies based only upon theory and conjecture. When the trial consists of multiple experts giving contradictory opinions based upon the same information, the expert's most important qualification may be the ability to give a convincing performance. Outstanding credentials and logical conclusions may be outweighed by the ability to present information in an easily understood manner. An examination before trial can be used to set the stage for an effective presentation.

Generally, unless there is advance agreement from the parties, an order from the court is necessary before proceeding with an opposing expert's deposition. If the court grants permission for the EBT, it usually does so upon condition that the expert be paid for time when testifying as well as time while preparing and reasonable travel expenses. If you are in any way an expert witness, and not a party to the lawsuit, you should not be shy about inquiring as to compensation when you receive the deposition notice.

8

ATTENDANCE IS MANDATORY

"Do I have to go?" you ask. Over the past several decades, we Americans have been busy cultivating our "let's not get involved" attitude. When faced with having to attend a deposition, some people try the avoidance approach, and hope it will go away if they just ignore it. It won't. Our courts are endowed with mighty powers to compel people to cooperate.

Rules about how much advance notice must be given to a witness differ throughout the country.

The first step in alerting a witness that he or she is wanted for a deposition is usually for a lawyer to send a notice stating the date, time, and place the witness must appear. Various jurisdictions have different rules about how much advance notice is required. Usually, unless there is a special order issued by the court, at least ten days notice is required. In California, witnesses get an additional day's notice for each 300 miles they must travel to the deposition site. Alaska, on the other hand, only requires that the witness be given "reasonable" notice.

IF YOU REFUSE

If a witness will not attend a deposition voluntarily, a subpoena summons may be served. The subpoena is equivalent to an order from the court that directs a witness to set aside everything else in daily life and appear when and where told. If the witness tries to ignore a subpoena, the court may take further steps to force compliance. The court may direct the police or sheriff to seek out and escort the witness to the proceedings. Beyond the embarrassment of having the police come looking for you, the court has the authority to impose other punishments on those who refuse to comply, including fines and even time in jail. Failing to obey a subpoena is punishable as contempt of court, and gives rise to criminal penalties.

Even leaving the country may not help. Most foreign courts will obey requests from American courts to compel the testimony of uncooperative witnesses. Most foreign governments will permit American consular officers to serve subpoenas on U.S. nationals, requiring them to return to the United States to testify.

Stiff fines, arrest, and jail time for contempt of court are some ways the court can force you to attend the deposition. The case can also be predecided against you if you refuse to co-operate.

Under the Federal Rules and the rules of many states, the court may impose other stiff sanctions upon someone who refuses to comply with a notice to appear at an examination before trial. The court can order that the offending party pay reasonable fees for failing to show up. These include such things as transportation costs, the court reporter's fee, and fees payable to the opposition attorneys.

If the person who refuses to be deposed is a party to the lawsuit, the court can preclude specific claims or defenses from being heard at the trial. In other words, the court can issue an order that prevents the offending party from introducing evidence at trial dealing with the matters that would have been covered at the deposition.

Similarly, the court can issue an order that the matters that would have been covered at the examination before trial, or any other designated matters, are deemed established. This means that it will not be necessary for the opposition to prove these things at trial. The jury will be told to consider the specific matters that would have been covered by the EBT to be established as fact against the offending party.

The court has other powers as well. It can postpone further proceedings until the witness complies. It can render a default judgment against a party who refuses to comply, and it can prevent the offending party from defending or prosecuting parts of the case.

Occasionally, a situation arises in which a witness prefers to receive a subpoena instead of simply complying with a deposition notice. For example, if your boss refuses to allow you time off from work, you may want to be served with a subpoena at your workplace so the boss knows you have no choice. A subpoena may also list documents or items you don't want to produce voluntarily. If you find yourself in these circumstances, discuss the situation immediately with your attorney.

Do You Get Paid?

Giving deposition testimony is considered a civic duty. Unless you qualify as an expert, you won't be paid for missing work or for the inconvenience. There may be special rules requiring that professionals be compensated for professional testimony, but for the average citizen the sole reward is the satisfaction of having advanced the public good by serving with only the noble motive of participating in the justice system.

Unless you qualify as an expert, there is usually no requirement that you will be paid for attending.

The Site

If you receive a notice to testify, your best bet is to cooperate. Sometimes, if the place specified in the notice is too inconvenient, the attorneys who serve the deposition notice will make other arrangements. If everyone cannot agree upon the place to hold the examination, the court will intervene when requested and make the decision itself. Some of the factors that a court will consider when designating the site for the EBT are: the distance the deponent will have to travel; the deponent's health and ability to get there; the expense involved in traveling to the deposition; the location of the forum where the lawsuit is pending (usually the county where the court is located); the location where other depositions in the case are being taken; the location and number of documents that may have to be produced; and the cost to the other parties of conducting the deposition at the requested location.

In one instance I recall, the vice president of a particular corporation refused to travel from Boston to Buffalo to give testimony in a case. He thought his time was too valuable. He submitted an affidavit to the court stating that he was willing to cooperate, but only if the deposition would be held in the corporate offices in Boston. After reading the affidavit, the judge ordered that the corporation pay all costs of the deposition if held in Boston, including the court reporter, transportation, overnight accommodations if necessary, and meals for the six lawyers representing the other parties in the lawsuit. After receiving the court order, the V.P. decided it would be more cost effective if he gave up his precious time and hopped on a plane to Buffalo.

Most judges like to be fair about these matters, and whenever possible, they will try to consider the convenience of witnesses. They will consider the importance of the potential testimony, too. In some cases,

Courts like to be fair about the deposition location and usually won't impose undue hardship on witnesses by forcing them to travel unreasonably.

they also will consider the amount in controversy. If the potential amount of damages to be awarded in the lawsuit is small, the court isn't likely to punish one of the parties by making them incur excessive expenses to travel to an examination before trial.

If a witness is unable to travel due to a medical condition, the site of the deposition may be changed. In cases of physical hardship or financial problems, the court will often require that the lawyers travel to where the witness is located, instead of having the witness travel to the EBT. For instance, a deposition of an injured or ill witness may be conducted in the witness's home. In extraordinary circumstances, the court may even permit the deposition to be conducted over a telephone line that is set up so that all of the lawyers and the court reporter can hear.

In some cases, the site of the deposition is selected to accommodate the type of testimony that will be given. For example, some lawsuits involve numerous documents and records. The records may need to be handy in case the witness must refer to them or in case questions about the documents arise during the testimony. It may be more appropriate to conduct the deposition in the warehouse where the records are kept instead of moving all of the files to another site for the deposition.

SCHEDULING

There is almost always some flexibility involved in scheduling the date and time for the deposition. If there is some pressing prior commitment, the date or time of the EBT can usually be changed. Courts expect lawyers to be courteous and to consider the convenience of witnesses and other attorneys when the deposition is scheduled. Of course, the lawyers are inclined to be less flexible if the time of the trial is rapidly approaching or if there has already been an order from the court to set the deposition date.

There is usually some flexibility in scheduling the deposition at a time convenient for all concerned.

There are ways to try to postpone or avoid depositions if you can get the court to agree. This requires a formal hearing in front of the judge, with notice of the hearing served upon all parties well in advance. Once in front of the judge, the lawyer representing the potential witness had better have a good reason for resisting. Judges don't like to preclude anyone from conducting an examination before trial, but they will issue orders to make the proceedings more acceptable. For instance, if the witness to be deposed is a child, the court may limit the time allowed, or direct that the deposition be conducted on a weekend or while school is out.

If the witness is not a party to the lawsuit, and if the witness is not represented by an attorney, a lawyer for one of the parties may contact the witness to discuss the case and explain the deposition procedure. In such cases, the witness and the lawyer can make arrangements for a convenient time to hold the deposition. If a subpoena is necessary, the lawyer and the witness can also arrange for the subpoena to be served in a manner that is convenient and that will save the witness from potential embarrassment.

IF YOU ARE SUBPOENAED

In most states, there are provisions to pay a fee to the witness when a subpoena is delivered. The fee is supposed to help defray the expenses of traveling to the deposition site. Most of the rules governing the amounts to be paid to witnesses are outdated. Witness fees, when paid, are really just a token to help ease the burden. A witness fee delivered with a subpoena usually won't even come close to covering the cab fare required to go to and from the examination.

If you receive an unexpected subpoena, and you have some questions about the proceedings, or an aversion to participating, check with your lawyer immediately. The first thing the attorney will determine is whether the subpoena is valid. If you haven't received the proper fee, or if the subpoena requires you to travel too far, immediate action may be necessary for your attorney to block it.

Your attorney can also take action to block a subpoena to prevent harrassment or to prevent having to provide information on trade secrets. Relief can be sought from the court to place limitations on what may be discovered, limit the number of persons who may be deposed, and prevent the deposition altogether if there is a more appropriate method (such as written questions) available for obtaining the required information.

Talk to your attorney immediately if you wish to discuss potential reasons to resist a subpoena.

9

THE PREPARATION SESSION

An examination before trial is like any other kind of test: You can improve your results with only a little preparation. The more you prepare, the better the chances that you will do well.

You should have at least one opportunity to sit down with your attorney and talk about the upcoming deposition. Based upon prior experience (yours and your attorney's) and the nature of the case, the attorney will best be able to determine how much preparation time you need.

Lawyers like to think of a preparation session as an opportunity to prepare the witness to testify, but the preparation session is also a chance for the witness to prepare the lawyer. Because you never quite know what to expect at the EBT, the preparation session should range far afield to properly prepare you, and to prepare your lawyer to handle your testimony.

The initial preparation session prepares both you and your lawyer.

Your lawyer will probably use some of the preparation time to educate you on the laws that pertain to the case. At the same time, you will be educating the attorney to understand the facts more clearly. Together, you and your attorney will determine what knowledge you have that is truly pertinent, and what topics need special attention for proper handling.

You and your lawyer will also take the opportunity to get to know each other a little better on a personal level. The lawyer can exercise better control over the proceedings if made aware of your special characteristics, and temperament, and natural constitution. Any unusual conditions, such as heart problems, lack of stamina, incontinence, memory difficulties, or medications should be discussed with your lawyer during the preparation session.

Since the lawyer's function at the deposition is partly to get the facts in order, it is important for you to have the opportunity to tell the lawyer all you know. The lawyer will then be in a better position to help you make a persuasive presentation. This is especially true if you have some technical knowledge or special expertise. In addition to advising the attorney of the facts of the case, you have the opportunity to make the lawyer familiar with technical words and jargon that may come up during the testimony. Since you will be required to explain things clearly during the deposition, the opportunity to explain things before hand to the attorney will serve as a sort of rehearsal to help you put your thoughts and words together.

TIMING

Ideally, the preparation session should take place well in advance of the deposition. The time gap between the preparation session and the deposition will give you extra time to investigate important details where information is lacking, or to assure yourself that your recollection is correct. It will also provide time, if necessary, to obtain further records or documents that may be essential to a successful examination before trial.

Don't schedule the preparation session so far in advance that you forget everything before the deposition.

Of course, the preparation session should not take place so far in advance that you forget everything you learn. I once heard a noted plaintiff's attorney comment that he prefers to cancel depositions at the last minute and reschedule them a few months later. He theorized that the opponent's witness would lose the benefit of the original preparation session and would not take the time to re-prepare. Depending on the complexity of the litigation and the level of preparation, it may be a good idea to have a second short session to review the initial preparation and reinforce EBT skills.

It has been said that, as in most sports, the majority of the lost points at a deposition are due to errors you make yourself and not due to some brilliant offensive move by the opposition. One of the principal goals of the lawyer representing a deponent is to prevent the witness from making critically harmful mistakes. Proper preparation is what will enable you and your lawyer to minimize the potential for error.

PRACTICE

One of the best possible exercises at a preparation session is to conduct a mock deposition. You and your attorney take the time to go through some of the most likely questions, giving you the opportunity to practice the kind of answers needed at the EBT. In order to give the case proper attention, the preparation session should not be rushed, and should be conducted in your attorney's office, in an environment that provides few interruptions and distractions. You should not try to do it over the phone or to squeeze it in between other commitments. It is too important not to plan ahead.

The best defense against a capable examining attorney is to come to the deposition thoroughly prepared. The importance of the examination before trial more than justifies whatever preparation time you and your lawyer have to put in.

A practice session with questions and answers will most effectively prepare you for giving testimony.

10

WHAT WILL THEY ASK?

The questions that arise at a deposition will, of course, depend on the subject matter of the lawsuit. Since no two lawsuits are ever exactly the same, nobody can predict exactly what the questions will be.

Our courts want to afford the parties as much access to evidence and information as possible, so the standard for questions that can be asked at a deposition is very broad. Information is considered discoverable if it can be related to the facts or legal issues of the case in any way. In addition to asking direct questions about the evidence, attorneys are permitted to ask indirect, and seemingly irrelevant, questions that are calculated to lead to other sources of evidence. This is a different standard of questioning than is allowed in the courtroom. Many questions are asked at an examination before trial that would not be asked at the trial itself.

The subject matter for deposition questions is generally broader than the subject matter that can be covered at trial.

BACKGROUND QUESTIONS

Even though all of the subjects for questioning cannot be predicted, there are certain areas of questioning that are common to most EBT's. There is almost always some questioning about the witness's background. This includes inquiry into past places of residence, level of education, and other life experience.

These background questions usually appear to novice witnesses to be quite innocent, until they understand how the attorney may attempt to use the information obtained. Often a witness will be questioned

The attorney will almost always ask about your background in detail.

about every place of residence since childhood. A complete employment history may be obtained, as well as information on prior names, military service, and even prior lawsuits.

Deposition witnesses usually view these questions as being totally irrelevant to the lawsuit at hand, and may even feel that some of the questions are silly. After all, what does it matter if I lived in New Hampshire for the last ten years (where the speed limit is 65), if I was injured in an expressway accident in a totally different state, New York (where the limit is lower), a few months after moving there?

The opposition attorneys will use the answers to the seemingly silly questions to do a background check to find collateral information about the witness that may be used at a trial. If the witness is an injured plaintiff, the defense has access to a computer system that lists every past insurance claim. The background of any witness can be checked for a criminal record, and information on prior residence addresses may be used to canvass the old neighborhoods for information. The higher the stakes in the litigation, the more important to find the weak spots in the opposing witnesses' armor.

RULES MAY CHANGE IN COURT

Attorneys can ask some types of questions at the deposition even though the information may not be used in court.

However, just because a question is asked during a deposition does not mean the information can be used in court. Attorneys are given broad latitude to ask questions while they are fishing around at the EBT, but they are still confined to the rules regarding relevancy of evidence at trial. It is up to the judge to decide whether the information obtained may be presented as part of the case in the courtroom.

During the course of the deposition, your lawyer may object "for the record" to certain questions that are asked, but that won't stop you from having to answer them. Since just about any seemingly insignificant subject appears to be fair game for the deposition, you had better be prepared for the fact that things you never thought would be revealed sometimes come out in the testimony.

11

SKELETONS IN THE CLOSET

Is there some past trouble lurking in your background that might return to haunt you? Have you done something embarrassing that you are reluctant to talk about? Even if you believe that some difficulty in your background has nothing to do with your case, you should discuss it, in private, with your attorney. Your attorney will be able to help you prepare for handling the unexpected things that might come out at a deposition.

PREPARE FOR AWKWARD QUESTIONS

In a case involving an automobile accident, I recently had the following exchange with the driver of the plaintiff's automobile:

> Q. Have you ever been convicted of a crime?
> A. Yes. Yeah.
> Q. When was that?
> A. Oh, let's see. '68, '80, '81—somewhere around there. I don't believe—I'm not sure—
> Q. More than once?
> A. Pardon.
> Q. Were you convicted more than once?
> A. Yes. I been arrested quite a few times but most of them was thrown out. A lot of them was dismissed and I got proba-

Answer all questions as narrowly as possible; don't provide any extra details.

> tion. I never served no time on none of them. I got proba-
> tion and fines.
> WITNESS'S ATTORNEY: He's not asking you those questions,
> okay. You do not have to volunteer.
> THE WITNESS: Okay.
> WITNESS'S ATTORNEY: Just answer the questions that he
> asks. Listen to what he's asking.

A criminal record may seem to have little to do with a lawsuit concerning an automobile accident. Then why did I ask the questions?
Because the rules of law specifically provide that a person who has
been convicted of a crime may be questioned on the subject, and that
the conviction may be brought out in a civil trial for the purpose of
affecting the weight of the witness's testimony. In other words, if you
have been convicted of a crime of moral turpitude (robbery, assault—
not just a parking fine), the judge and jury are allowed to take that into
consideration when they decide whether they are going to believe what
you say in the courtroom.

However, as you can see in the above example, an unprepared
witness can give the opposing attorney plenty of extra ammunition if
not ready for the question. The question I asked this particular witness
concerned prior convictions. Instead of answering about a conviction,
the witness started telling me about being "arrested quite a few times."
His attorney finally stepped in and made him aware that there is a difference in the eyes of the law between being convicted and merely
arrested.

If he had been prepared to handle the question properly, I might
have come away from the deposition with the impression that this witness was convicted one time, given a fine and probation, and learned
his lesson. Instead, I came away with the impression that this witness
was some kind of career criminal, and that this lawsuit may have been
just another scam planned to make an easy buck.

ANYTHING MIGHT COME UP

One of the most surprising exchanges I have heard concerned a witness's hidden background in another negligence case. I was listening to

the plaintiff's attorney examine the owner of the codefendant's company in regard to how the codefendant had conducted a clean-up operation at the site where the plaintiff was injured. When the witness was questioned about his background, the following became part of the record:

> Q. Have you ever been convicted of a crime?
>
> A. Speeding ticket.
>
> WITNESS'S ATTORNEY: That's not a crime.
>
> WITNESS: It isn't?
>
> WITNESS'S ATTORNEY: No.
>
> WITNESS: No crimes.
>
> PLAINTIFF'S ATTORNEY: Are you a veteran?
>
> A. Yes, I am.
>
> Q. And did you receive an honorable discharge?
>
> A. Never got one.
>
> Q. You're still in the service?
>
> A. Well, it's like this, I was in the 102nd field artillery, and it was just a bad situation. I went out of my way to make vehicles run and it was not my echelon of maintenance, and a General broke me to a Private after I was a Master Sargeant, and the battalion commander, my Captain, gave me the money to go to town to buy civilian parts to put in an Army vehicle, and then wouldn't stand behind me. So I told them do what you want to do, I quit and I come home, and I never got no discharge.

Plan ahead for awkward questions about your background.

Instead of voluntarily admitting to being AWOL from the armed services, the witness could have found a much better way to treat the subject. Unfortunately, he obviously didn't prepare with his attorney by discussing the embarrassing tale before the EBT. If he had, his attorney would undoubtedly have helped him out.

The attorney might have objected to the relevancy of the subject matter, forcing the opposition to obtain a court order before the question was answered. The opposition might not have bothered going to the trouble of getting a court order and scheduling a further deposition, since the subject matter wasn't really relevant to the case.

The attorney might also have helped his witness form a strategic answer. For example, when asked about his discharge, the witness might merely have made a snide remark such as, "I'm no longer in the army, you can probably tell from the uniform." This stab, almost as if to say to the opposition's attorney "dumb question," might well have thrown the attorney off the track. Attorneys don't want to appear to be asking dumb questions on the record. This kind of tactical response often works where the subject of the question is not germain to the facts of the lawsuit. If the particular area of questioning is not very important, and not likely to be the subject of further in-depth investigation, the witness may be able to hide the skeleton altogether by throwing off the interrogator with an unanticipated response.

If, after receiving such a tactical response, the questioning attorney tried to pursue the matter a little further, the witness could probably have put the matter to rest by saying "I was not dishonorably discharged from the service, if that's what you mean." After all, that would have been a true statement. The opposing attorney, not thinking that there could be another alternative (such as never being discharged), would probably have figured that the witness received an honorable discharge, and would have gone on to another subject for questioning.

THE TRUTH IS BEST

Don't volunteer extra information, but do always tell the truth.

You must never be merely obstructive. It is important to satisfy the legal requirement of responding with full disclosure, and it's best not to give the impression that you're holding something back. Besides that, both you and your attorney may be subject to court sanctions, including stiff fines, if you fail to cooperate. In addition, failing to disclose information that the opposition may find out about later (such as a record of past criminal convictions) can lead to scathing commentary at trial, which could be ruinous to your case.

There is a difference, however, between being obstructive and volunteering harmful information. The trick here is to anticipate the opponent's use of the information, anticipate the question, and prepare a tactical response. However, if there is no way to get around it, **the truth will probably hurt less at a deposition than it will if it comes out unexpectedly at trial.**

Confronting the truth may cause the opposition to be impressed by your directness and openness. It also provides the opportunity to develop a good rationale to help explain the problem in a more favorable light. Even if the truth is uncomfortable, it is much better to have it come out at an EBT so that you have the opportunity to deal with it, than to have an opponent find out the secret by some other means and use the information to drop a bomb on you at the trial.

12

PRIOR STATEMENTS

A common skeleton in the litigant's closet is the spectre of prior statements. Attorneys, insurance companies, and governmental agencies often try to get the jump on litigation by interviewing witnesses and parties before a lawsuit is filed.

An insurance company representative, or an investigator hired by one of the parties, may take a statement from a witness years before the formal litigation begins. Although the witness may have thought that the talk was off the record at the time, it can easily become part of the record when referred to later at the deposition. "By the way, Mr. Witness, didn't you tell the investigator, Mr. So-and-So, a few years ago, that . . . ?"

These statements are sometimes recorded over the phone, or in person, and sometimes just exist in the form of notes taken by the investigator during a conversation. Prior statements also exist in the form of written materials generated by the witness.

For example, in one noncompetition case we litigated a few years ago, we obtained copies of loan applications and written notes that were taken by a bank's loan officer when the defendant made an application to finance his new business. These records clearly showed that the defendant had not only been planning to compete with our client, his former employer, but that he had been bragging to the bank about the inside information from our client's company that he planned to use.

It's no wonder that lawyers often tell their clients not to talk to anyone about the case. A prior statement may be problematic for a number of reasons. A cunning investigator may try to put words in the witness's mouth, or the witness may have been misinformed at the time the state-

Don't discuss the case with anyone but your attorney. If you have made statements to anyone, let your lawyer know.

ment was made. The witness may also have had a better memory of the situation at the time the statement was given and may be mixed up about the details when called upon to testify years later. The contradictory statements are often used to weaken a witness's credibility.

Worst of all, the witness may have lied or exaggerated when the statement was given. If it wasn't a statement under oath, the witness may not have thought much of it, and may have given no thought to the possibility that the words could be the cause of future regret.

The good news is that, in most jurisdictions, you are entitled to see copies of any prior statements you made before testifying. If warned in advance, your attorney will have the opportunity to try to get copies of statements obtained by the opposition, or statements in the hands of an independent source, to review in preparing for the deposition.

Here's an example from a Pennsylvania case of a witness who had given some previous answers while connected to a lie detector. This unfortunate witness forgot to have his attorney obtain copies of all of his prior statements before the deposition:

Q. Did you see Sharlene Wilson driving a car that evening?

A. No, I didn't.

Q. Do you know what kind of a car Sharlene Wilson was driving that evening?

A. No, I don't.

Q. Have you since come to know what type of car she was driving that evening?

A. No.

Q. The polygraph examiner asked you several questions when you took a polygraph test, and at this point I would like to ask you to address the answers that you made to several questions. The polygraph examiner asked you: "What were you thinking when I asked you the question just now, could you take me to the car that forced Sharlene off the road?" That's the question that the polygraph examiner asked you, and the polygraph examiner noted here your answer as: "I'm wondering, because of the way I drove down the road that night, if I am the one that forced her off the road." Did you make that statement to the polygraph examiner?

WITNESS'S ATTORNEY: Objection.

WITNESS: Yes, I may have.

PLAINTIFF'S ATTORNEY: The same night as the accident?

WITNESS: Can I talk to him for a minute?

PLAINTIFF'S ATTORNEY: Let the record reflect that the witness is speaking to his attorney off the record.

WITNESS'S ATTORNEY: Let the record also reflect that he does have a right to speak to counsel, doesn't he?

PLAINTIFF'S ATTORNEY: Sure, I just want the fact of the private consultation at this point to be on the record.

WITNESS: I forget what his question was.

WITNESS'S ATTORNEY: Do you want to go outside?

WITNESS: Yeah.

(RECESS)

(PENDING QUESTION READ BACK)

PLAINTIFF'S ATTORNEY: Are you saying here today that you are no longer wondering whether or not Sharlene was driving and that you're no longer wondering whether you were driving a car that caused her to go off the road?

WITNESS: That's correct.

Q. And why is that?

A. I know myself, you know, down in my heart that it wasn't me and that it never happened.

Q. Why? Is there—

A. Why?

Q. I'm not trying to be tricky here. I'm just—You were wondering about it when you gave the statement to the polygraph examiner, and I have a copy of his notes here that I can show you and your attorney. Pass these over. You were wondering back then, now you're not wondering. Back then it was closer to the time of the accident. What has happened between then and now that convinces you that you were not the one driving the car that forced her off the road?

A. I believe when they had that lie detector on me, I was upset.

Q. And you're not upset now. Well, maybe you should be.

WITNESS'S ATTORNEY: Objection.

Another kind of prior statement exists in the form of written legal documents, such as pleadings and answers to written interrogatories. Although these documents are drafted by attorneys, litigants usually have to sign them to verify that the contents are alleged to be true. You will want to familiarize yourself with the contents of any such statements you made before you are questioned about them at a deposition.

HOW YOUR LAWYER CAN HELP

The more lead time, the better your lawyer can help you prepare to deal with past problems.

Where matters of truthfulness are concerned, clients are sometimes confused about the role their attorney is supposed to play. The attorney is not supposed to win the case at all costs. In some situations, an attorney may even have a duty to the court to produce the "smoking gun," and he may have to do so even if it is very hurtful to his client's cause. Information about a destroyed document, or a prior accident with similar circumstances, may have to come out whether the litigant likes it or not. What the lawyer can and will do is help minimize the potential damage.

The deposition preparation session is sometimes the first face-to-face meeting between the deponent and the lawyer where there is a serious detailed discussion about the case. At that time, in an isolated environment, you should have ample opportunity to explore the private facts before they become public. However, if there is a ticklish subject you expect may come up, there is no reason to wait before alerting your lawyer. It may take considerable thought and preparation to find the best way to deal with the problem. It can take weeks, or even months, to obtain copies of prior statements or to ferret out other proof or disproof of skeletons in the closet. The best approach is to tell your lawyer about potential problems as soon as possible.

13

GETTING ORGANIZED

There is usually plenty of time available to prepare for the deposition. The law requires that advance notice be given to the person who is going to be deposed. Also, because it is difficult to arrange a time when several lawyers and witnesses can conveniently convene, it is quite common for the examination before trial to be postponed—perhaps several times—before the proceeding actually takes place.

Nevertheless, once you are notified that a deposition has been scheduled, you should begin to get organized immediately. This will save time and confusion on the day of the deposition, and will go a long way toward helping you to be a better witness. Take time to organize your thoughts as well as any evidence you may be presenting.

ORGANIZING YOUR THOUGHTS

Organizing your thoughts requires that you take the time for one or two thought sessions to seriously contemplate the matters that are likely to be the subject of the lawsuit.

It is surprising how may people, confronted with what they may consider the odious prospect of attending a deposition, put off thinking about the whole thing until they arrive at the attorney's office. Because of this procrastination, they do not have the information they will need fresh in their minds, and they are not prepared to give accurate testimony.

To help you pre-pare, set aside some private time to think about the case.

Set aside an hour or so to prepare your mind. Sit somewhere quiet, perhaps with your favorite drink handy, and let everyone know you are not to be disturbed. Then relax, and think back.

The best way to organize your thoughts is usually to approach the subject in chronological order. Think first about the background of the subject matter, and then the events leading up to whatever it was that caused the lawsuit. Then think about whatever transpired afterward.

Try to iron out the details in your own mind, without guessing or making assumptions. If there are things that you don't know, make a mental note to find out, or at least be aware that there are areas where your knowledge is lacking so that you will be able to discuss this with your attorney.

Thought sessions will work best if you take the time well in advance of the deposition, when there is little or no pressure to get ready. To keep the ideas fresh in your memory, it is best to engage in another short thought review session the day before you are scheduled to testify.

No Notes Unless Necessary

Particularly in complicated cases, you may be inclined to jot down a few notes or thoughts to help you with your testimony. This may be dangerous. **Be careful not to rely on your notes.** You do not want them to become a crutch, and your attorney will not want you to refer to your notes when you testify. It may also cause you difficulty if the other side discovers that the notes exist.

You will make a much better impression upon the opposition if you are able to recall things from memory. They will recognize that tes-timony is more effective in front of a judge and jury when spoken from your own mind and not from written notes.

Stick to easily remembered men-tal notes rather than written notes.

Even more important is the fact that **If you use notes to refresh your recollection, you may have to give your notes to the opposi-tion.** The rules of discovery are broadly interpreted to allow your opponents access to whatever materials you use or refer to when testi-fying.

If you must make notes to prepare your testimony, give them to your attorney, and do not take them into the deposition room with you. You can imagine how harmful it might be if you had to refer to your notes to answer a question, and because you looked at them, ended up turning your notes over to the opposition. It would be especially harmful if your notes included information the opposition would not otherwise have obtained.

Often, a sharp opposition attorney will ask you if you have made any writings regarding the case to help refresh your memory. If you have made written notes, it is good to remember that notes do not have to be disclosed if they are intended for your attorney as a personal communication. There is a difference in the eyes of the law between merely keeping a diary or writing a narrative report and writing something specifically for your attorney to read. Communications prepared for your attorney are usually considered privileged, which means they are not subject to discovery by the other side. The same applies to any tape recordings you make. If you are going to make notes in preparation for your testimony, you may want to address them in the form of a letter directed to your lawyer. Then, if you are asked whether you have made any writings, you can testify that you only made written communications for your attorney. This will preclude any further questioning on the matter.

ORGANIZING EVIDENCE

Lawsuits usually involve some form of documents, files, papers, or other evidence. These may include something simple, such as an interoffice memorandum, a written accident report, a series of bills and cancelled checks, a lease or other contract, or a set of photographs. More complex cases can involve rooms full of company records, design plans, and schematic diagrams.

Witnesses usually have to refer to a file or document to identify the probative evidence (portions of evidence that prove the case) or to remember certain detailed information when they testify. However, it can be embarrassing and disconcerting, and can possibly damage your credibility if you have to fumble around through stacks of materials trying to find the answer to a simple question.

Searching through papers is almost always necessary to some extent, and the lawyers will be somewhat patient. However, you should be able to obtain the required information in a reasonable amount of time. If it takes too long to extract the needed evidence, you may

Organize papers and other evidence in advance to prevent the embarrassment and distraction of having to fumble around.

become unnerved. A disorganized witness runs the risk of starting to panic and completely losing the ability to concentrate.

To avoid this, take the time to organize records before the deposition. Few people keep their filing systems completely organized. Many different types of documents may be lumped together under one broad subject heading. If you have a lot of records to deal with at the deposition, it is best to separate things out and organize files using appropriate subdivisions. This will permit you to move efficiently from one piece of evidence to the next.

Coming to the examination before trial with your papers organized will not only make your job of testifying easier, it also enhances your image as a serious, intelligent individual in the eyes of everyone present. If you take the time to get organized, you will naturally look more professional and sophisticated, which will greatly add to your credibility as a witness.

14

DRESS TO IMPRESS

The image you will convey at the deposition involves much more than your testimony. Your physical appearance is extremely important. You can be the best prepared witness in the world and still not make the right impression if you don't look the part.

Before deciding what to wear to the examination, consult your attorney and determine the type of image you wish to portray. Since you never get a second chance to make a first impression, considerable thought must be given to clothing, makeup, jewelry, and accoutrements.

For example, if you are supposed to be an expert in accounting, you will want to dress the way an accountant is expected to dress. Just because you have taken the day off from work to attend the deposition is no reason to come casually attired.

The manner in which you are dressed may be determined by the purpose of the deposition. For instance, if the deposition is being held as part of a bankruptcy proceeding to determine what your assets are (so that the opposition creditors can decide whether to pursue your personal holdings, or just to take what they can get and settle), you may want to avoid wearing your usual gold neckchain and diamond rings.

Plaintiffs should not appear wealthy if they are trying to elicit sympathy. Defendants should not appear poor and disheveled when trying to show that they are upright citizens.

The colors you wear also have an effect. Every man's wardrobe should have a "sincere" tie (usually maroon). This is the time to wear it. Women should stay away from extremes in style or loud colors. Heavy colognes and perfumes should also be avoided.

Different styles of dress may be appropriate for different types of lawsuits, but in general plan on neat conservative attire.

Even hairstyle can come into play. If you attend the deposition with a hairstyle that went out of fashion many years ago, you may create the impression that you're generally unaware of your surroundings. Of course, under some circumstances, you may be "playing dumb," and an out-of-date look may be exactly what your lawyer wants you to achieve. As a general rule, neat conservative attire is in order. The deposition is not a time to express your creativity and eccentricity. It is a time to put aside your personal taste in favor of making the proper impression.

15

THE EXAMINATION STARTS BEFORE YOU ARRIVE

Don't wait until you are actually in the deposition room to get into the proper frame of mind. Some witnesses have the misfortune of giving their case away before the formal proceedings begin.

BE DISCREET

Be aware that statements you make to friends or other nonparties can come back to haunt you. Even though you may not seriously mean what you say, it is better to stay in the habit of not discussing the case with anyone except your lawyer.

In a case involving a physical injury, for example, the injured person should be prepared to be watched by the opposition at all times. It simply won't do to walk from the parking lot to the building carrying your crutches, and then walk into the deposition room using them. Similarly, I once had a person courteously open doors for me, only to find out later that I was the attorney who was about to question him about his alleged debilitating hand injury. It became a little silly when he tried to claim at the examination before trial that his wrist was so badly injured he had trouble turning door knobs.

Most importantly, learn to keep your mouth shut on the way to the deposition. I have had more than one experience riding up in elevators

Be careful not to do or say anything before the deposition that can harm your case.

listening to witnesses foolishly discuss their cases. Had they known that the attorney for the other side was standing right behind them, they would probably not have discussed the matter in my presence. So why take a chance discussing cases in front of a group of strangers?

Waiting rooms are not places to be overly sociable either. Don't try to make friends, don't apologize, and don't discuss your personal affairs with anyone. Greet the opposition pleasantly, or matter-of-factly, and do nothing more. It's best not to exchange any words other than a simple greeting.

NOTE WHAT THE OPPOSITION SAYS

Be mindful of clues that emanate from the opposition and bring them to your lawyer's attention.

On the other hand, you will want to tell your attorney about any remarks you hear the opposition make. If the opponent says something like "I'm sorry" out in the waiting room, or makes a statement such as "This isn't going to get me anywhere," or somebody says "I can't believe we're going through all of this for a measly $10,000," your attorney will want to know. Knowledge of such comments may supply some extra ammunition for your attorney to use when examining the opposition witness or in later negotiations.

Winners don't wait until they are sworn in to start defending themselves. If your position in the litigation is worth defending at all, it is worth being conscientious about at all times.

16

DEALING WITH DEPOSITION ANXIETY

Some amount of anxiety always accompanies the prospect of testifying at an examination before trial. The best way to handle such fear is to identify it and deal with it. The following are some of the most common causes of apprehension.

"THESE PEOPLE AREN'T GOING TO LIKE ME"

Beginning with childhood, we develop an image of the acceptable, likable person, and the need to be accepted and liked ourselves. Although involved in a lawsuit, every person still wants to be liked. The witness wants to be liked by everyone at the deposition, and more importantly, wants to think that if the case goes to trial, the judge and the jury will also be enchanted.

It is absurd to believe that anyone can be liked universally. To paraphrase an outstanding trial attorney of old, you will be liked by some of the people some of the time, and most of the people some of the time, but don't expect everyone at the deposition to be pleased.

It isn't necessary for everyone, or in fact anyone, at the deposition to like you. It won't be necessary at trial for every member of the jury to like you either. This is a lawsuit, not a popularity contest. The people involved are trying to figure out what the facts are. They are not trying to make a decision about whether to invite you to their next cocktail party.

A deposition is not a popularity contest. You need to make a good impression, but not to make everyone like you.

"This is Too Important, I Can't Handle It"

Take the time to prepare—then do the best you can.

While it is true that the deposition is important, if you attach too much importance to it, you run the risk of making yourself so anxious that you may not be able to function when it comes time to testify. Instead of worrying about how important the deposition may be, a better approach would be to take the time to prepare and then resolve to just do the best you can. In reality, that is all anyone can ask of you.

"I'm Afraid I'll Blow It"

Most people have a fear of being in any sort of spotlight with attention focused on them. Some people carry with them the experience of public embarrassment for the rest of their lives. Stage fright is normal.

Keep in mind that everyone at the deposition is probably nervous—including the lawyers! This kind of anxiety is most easily assuaged by developing an understanding of what is really expected of you.

You aren't expected to put on a polished performance—minor errors are normal.

You are **not** expected to be perfect. You are **not** expected to put on a polished performance. You are expected to make a few normal mistakes. Everyone fumbles over words or becomes confused from time to time. These blunders are part of every examination before trial, and are rarely fatal to the case.

"I Hate Conflict"

If you're the kind of person who likes to avoid conflict in your life (most sane people are like that), then there will naturally be some anxiety when you have to face a situation that inherently involves disagreement. Some people actually give up on lawsuits altogether, just to avoid the conflict.

Don't give up just because there is a disagreement—ironing out disagreements is what the system is all about.

If you think about it, you will realize that some degree of conflict exists in your life every day. Unless you are a hermit, conflict is part of daily society. Thinking that you can avoid conflict, or that problems will just go away, is foolish.

Instead of thinking about avoiding the conflict, you should welcome it. This is going to be a learning experience, and you will probably be a better and wiser person for having gone through it.

"They Won't Believe Me"

Most people faced with a deposition have a natural tendency to become defensive. You know your veracity will be questioned and, as a result, you might feel that everything you say must somehow be justified further.

Becoming defensive during an examination before trial tends to make you look guilty, even if you're not. If you spend too much time trying to make explanations, it will appear as though you are making excuses.

Try to understand that you are testifying because you have the knowledge. You are the only one who knows what you know. That is what you are going to testify about. If you speak from the heart, with energy and clarity, you will appear believable.

> Some people won't be convinced no matter what you say, but that shouldn't prevent you from telling your side of the story.

If you aren't believed by everyone, don't let it bother you. Just as some of the people will be predisposed to believe your side of the story, some people are going to be predisposed not to believe what you say, and no matter what comes out, they won't act convinced. This is perfectly natural. After all, if there weren't more than one possible side of the story, there wouldn't be any need for a lawsuit to begin with.

"I Might Have to Say Something Nasty about Someone, and I Don't Want to Get Into Trouble"

Deponents often wonder if they can be sued for libel or slander because of something they say at a deposition. The answer is no. Provided that the statement has some reasonable relation or reference to the subject of the litigation, witnesses generally have absolute immunity whenever a statement is made in the course of a judicial proceeding. Additionally, communications between witnesses and counsel,

> Your testimony is generally immune from libel or slander claims.

written pleadings, and depositions, even though not actually made in a courtroom, are generally immune from a defamation claim.

"I Can't Deal With the Complexity"

Provided you are prepared and take your time, even the most complex cases eventually unfold in a somewhat organized manner. Most cases, when pared down to their significant details, aren't really very complex at all. Don't forget that the attorneys figure they are going to eventually have to explain this case to a court. They are going to try their best to sort the facts and create order out of the chaos so that the pertinent details will be easy to grasp.

The deposition process helps you sort out the complex details of the case.

Everyone hates to admit they have weaknesses. Everyone fears a bad performance. But a scared witness can become an unthinking and unconvincing witness if the usual, normal anxiety is allowed to be blown out of proportion.

Try to keep in mind that the court, whether judge or jury, is also composed of human beings. Human beings tend to identify with one another. Judges, jurors, attorneys, and other parties all identify with witnesses. They understand the witnesses' needs and fears, because they have similar needs and fears themselves.

When you are called to testify as a witness, it is because you know more about what you are going to say than anyone else on earth. Don't be afraid to be called upon to say it.

17

THE DEPOSITION ROOM

Most depositions are conducted in a library or conference room, around a large table, or in one of the attorneys' offices. Depending on the number of litigants involved and the number of witnesses to be questioned, the deposition room can be crowded and uncomfortable.

If the examination before trial is conducted in the attorney's office, the attorney who summoned you will probably sit behind a desk while asking the questions. This allows the attorney to exude the impression of power. The rest of the lawyers and witnesses will find chairs angled toward the desk. In a conference room or library, there is usually a very large table. The opposing sides will face each other across the table, and the court reporter will sit at one end.

Deposition rooms are often crowded and uncomfortable.

Wherever the deposition is held, it is important for the reporter to be able to see the faces of the witnesses and hear the testimony clearly. If more than one witness is to testify, the witnesses and attorneys may change seats so the reporter can hear and see clearly.

ENTER THE ROOM EARLY

There are certain advantages to being the first to enter the deposition room. The room itself often provides an intimidating atmosphere. If it serves as a library, it may be filled with old dusty law books. It may also be filled with expensive-looking furniture. Whatever the atmosphere, it will certainly be foreign to you and therefore somewhat uncomfortable. Most litigants find the deposition room close and claustrophobic.

Arrive at the room a little early, if possible, to help feel settled in.

The party who must testify first may not have the time to become acclimated to the surroundings. If you can be in the room a little early, you will have the opportunity to look around, to choose a seat, and to settle in.

THE ATMOSPHERE

Lawyers spend lots of money on their law libraries and conference rooms. They do this to impress clients as much as to provide themselves with an adequate work atmosphere. I often hear witnesses comment about the books when they first enter a library-deposition room. The shelves of law books make an immediate impression. So do large conference tables and works of art.

The more you know about lawyers, the more you come to realize that, although they are usually smart and well-educated, they are often educated merely in the academic sense. Many lawyers lack street smarts. That is, they spend so much time in a limited academic environment that they lack the valuable background of a broader experience.

Nevertheless, the lawyer's game is often one of intimidation. They will take the "smarter than you" attitude, and hang their diplomas on the wall in expensive frames as a way of showing their smarts, even though they may be particularly uneducated in the basics that will be important to the particular litigation.

Never mind the plush surroundings; concentrate on the task at hand.

If you understand that their conference room, library, and fancy office are all part of the game, then they lose some of their power to intimidate. If you understand that the surroundings look expensive because the attorney is trying to convey the impression of success, whether the attorney in fact owns or leases the furniture or is in danger of having it repossessed—then you also come to realize that the lawyer who has placed you in this fearful environment is also merely human. Lawyers have the same problems trying to achieve success that everyone else has.

If the deposition is conducted in a library room, rest assured that the lawyer hasn't read all of the law books that line the walls, and probably hasn't even opened most of them. They are research tools. The books are there for the attorney to refer to if a question comes up from the court or a client. There's an old adage that goes, "Lawyers aren't supposed to know the answers, they're just supposed to know how to find the answers." Most likely, no one will be doing any research or consulting any of those dusty old law books during the deposition.

Most of the books are obsolete anyway.

18

CHOOSING A SEAT

If you have the opportunity to choose your seat in the deposition room, you can do a few things that may work to your advantage. You may also be able to politely insist upon changing seats when it is your turn to testify, if for some reason you are not comfortable with the situation.

Don't be afraid to ask to change your seat if you aren't comfortable.

WINDOWS AND GLASS WALLS

If there are windows in the room, try to sit with your back to them. Windows can be distracting. Staring into the light for hours on end also creates eyestrain and fatigue. If the lawyer questioning you has her back to the light, you won't be able to see her face clearly. You will be more easily intimidated. It will feel like an old movie, where you are a spy and the enemy is attempting to break your will by shining a light in your eyes. Not only is it exhausting to be straining under the light, but if you can't see the face of the person asking the questions, you can't tell what she is up to, and you can't be sure you are looking her straight in the eyes when you answer.

Use the light in the room to your advantage. Let the lawyer squint as she tries to see **your** face. If there are no windows in the room, and certain areas of the table are better lit than others, keep in mind that you may be shown some exhibits or have to identify some evidence. Sit where the light will best suit your needs.

Whenever possible, sit with your back to the window and use the light in the room to your advantage.

Beware of the possible disadvantages of being assigned to sit in a certain place. These disadvantages can be both physical and psychological. For example, a smart attorney knows that by positioning himself between the witness and the door, he can create a slight feeling of entrapment in the mind of the witness. In doing so, the lawyer hopes the witness will feel psychologically controlled.

Some conference rooms, especially those installed in modern or remodeled offices, have a glass wall. This creates a nice picture-window effect to impress clients who may walk past the room and see the beautiful conference facilities or shelves of imposing law books. Unfortunately, although it looks nice from the outside looking in, it can be extremely distracting if you are facing the glass from the inside and watching people walk by while you're supposed to be paying attention to the proceedings. Sit with your back to the glass wall.

YOUR CHAIR

Pick a comfortable chair to increase your stamina during a long deposition.

If there is a choice, choose a comfortable chair. It is surprising how people enter a deposition room as if there is going to be a dinner party and the host will tell them where to be seated. Politeness has its place, but not if it's going to have a major effect on your ability to hold up under fire. Depositions can go on for hours. If you're sitting on a hard chair while you are testifying, or if you're uncomfortable while you are listening to the other parties and awaiting your turn, you are going to lose some of your physical stamina. Chairs that wobble and creak can also be embarrassing or distracting.

OTHER DISTRACTIONS

Be aware of other factors that may affect the environment in the deposition room. I was once in a room that had no windows and a noisy air-conditioning unit mounted on the wall. There was a pile of research material at one end of the conference table, because another lawyer had been using the room to do a research project. Instead of clearing the table, the host attorney set up the deposition at the other end of the room, directly under the noisy air conditioner. As the testimony began, it became clear that the court reporter was having trouble hearing the questions and answers. Nothing is more distracting than having the reporter, or one of the attorneys, stop you in midsentence to ask if a part of a question or part of an answer can be repeated.

Since one aspect of your role as a witness is to listen to the testimony of other witnesses, it may be just as important for you to hear what is going on as it is for you to testify. Watch out for seats near noisy heaters or air conditioners, or seats near an open door where there may be noisy distractions. There are even people who are sensitive to the high-pitched noise given off by certain types of fluorescent lights.

The time to take notice of a dripping faucet in your home is before you get into bed and pull up the covers for the night. If you don't notice it first, you will not only be aggravated by the sound, you will be doubly aggravated because you did not notice the annoyance before you got comfortable. Similarly, in the deposition room, the time to take notice of potential distractions is before you settle in.

Be sure you are seated so that you can hear, and aren't disadvantaged by other distractions in the room.

There are other reasons why lawyers choose to place witnesses in certain parts of the room. As already mentioned, positioning in relationship to the door can be used to control and intimidate. Conversely, if the lawyer wants to put the witness at ease, the witness may purposely be positioned nearer to the door. A certain position may also be chosen to prevent the witness from walking around the table and viewing notes or documents when entering the room.

In most cases, your lawyer will be sitting close by during your testimony. One of the roles your lawyer plays during a deposition is to provide you with moral support. He is a familiar face in the room. If there is a problem with where you are sitting, do not be afraid to let your lawyer know. Don't let the other side relegate you to an uncomfortable position in the deposition room, whether they are doing so on purpose or by accident. Your testimony is too important to start out at a disadvantage.

19

THE OFFENSIVE GAME PLAN

"He was the mildest mannere'd man that ever
scuttled ship or cut a throat."

Byron, Don Juan

Different lawyers have developed different styles of questioning. Some lawyers appear to have no style at all, which in itself may be considered a style. Even though it may seem that the lawyer is conducting a casual conversation, you can be sure that the manner of questioning was not planned in a casual way. You may also be surprised to see how, during the course of the deposition, the lawyer's deportment and mannerisms change drastically, without warning.

Styles of questioning may be broken down into two basic categories. The first is the questioner who is nice to the witness, and the second is the questioner who is antagonistic. Both styles of questioning have separate strategic purposes.

"NICE" LAWYERS

The questioner who is being overly nice is attempting to get the witness to relax. Strategically, the questioner is attempting to give the witness a false sense of security, almost to the point of pretending to be on the witness's side. If the lawyer becomes overly polite, allows plenty of

Some opposition attorneys will start the questioning in a pleasant manner, and then change to more aggressive tactics.

time, and exudes an atmosphere of repose and contentment with the answers, the witness is very likely being set up for a fall.

The ultra-polite lawyer waits for the witness to become relaxed and hopes the witness will volunteer some item of information or explanation. Tactically, the lawyer is hoping that the witness will climb out on a limb by tossing off a casual comment that can be used to the opponent's advantage.

Once the witness trips up, the lawyer will zero in on something the witness has said. Skillfully probing for more information, the questioning lawyer then begins to change mannerisms. There is a sudden appearance of belligerence. Interrogation comes more vigorously. Needless to say, the witness always finds this extremely disconcerting.

> "Things were going so nicely . . . and all of a sudden, the attorney got mad,"
>
> "When he started getting upset, I got rattled."
>
> "He started looking at me like I was lying."
>
> "I thought he was agreeing with me until I got to the part about . . . I probably should have said it differently."

These are typical comments from witnesses who have experienced an examination before trial in which the opposing attorney started with the overly nice strategy. These kinds of comments usually come from a witness who is paying too much attention to how the questions are asked, instead of concentrating on the content of the questions themselves.

ANTAGONISTIC ATTORNEYS

At times, the attorney may skip the nice approach and start with what appears to be a hostile attack. When the attorney uses this strategy, each question sounds like a personal affront. The questioner trys to put terror into the interrogation. Preliminary questions are asked in an accusatory tone of voice, even though the subject matter has little or nothing to do with the lawsuit. Pressure is put on the witness at every opportunity. Detail after detail is insisted upon, and an attempt is made to make the witness appear foolish at every turn.

Attorneys use different deposition styles for a reason. As mentioned in an earlier chapter, one of the main reasons for holding an examination before trial is to pretest the witnesses. The lawyers get more out of the deposition than just the spoken information. The opportunity is used to see how the witnesses will hold up under fire.

A lawyer who browbeats a witness is trying to determine what will happen if the same thing is done to the witness at trial. Will the witness become defensive? Will the witness fight back sarcastically? Will the witness get upset and start to say things he or she doesn't mean to say? Will the witness become uncooperative or react in some other way that a jury wouldn't like? Will the witness become just plain mixed up, giving the attorney some additional ammunition?

The lawyer's style of questioning is usually a test to see how you will hold up under fire in the courtroom.

Keep the Purpose in Mind

The best way to handle an attorney who appears antagonistic, condescending, or disrespectful is not to be antagonistic, condescending, or disrespectful in return. Instead, keep the lawyer's true purpose in the back of your mind. You know what's really going on, so play along with the game. Remain courteous. Be patient. Don't get upset no matter how vicious, slanderous, or accusatory you may feel the lawyer is trying to be. Just answer the questions that are asked, take the deposition seriously, and remain calm.

If you know that someone may be trying to trick you emotionally, it is easy to take a step back and remain relatively unemotional. This can be a tremendous advantage at a deposition.

If you feel you are being attacked, your first reaction will naturally be to go on the defensive. A better approach would be to say to yourself, "It isn't me personally that's under attack here; it is what I am saying that is under attack."

As an opposing witness, you are standing in the way of the lawyer who is trying to establish a client's case. Without a doubt, the lawyer will be displeased with some of your answers. The lawyer has to test some of those opposing answers to see if they will hold up. The lawyer must try to gain some control of the case by trying to gain some control over you when you testify.

Don't be tricked emotionally by what appears to be a hostile attack—expect that your answers will be tested.

Concentrate on Composure

You don't want to answer questions in a monotone with a blank look on your face. You want to be natural. You want to impress the attorneys with your honesty and openness. But you also want the questioning attorney to leave the deposition with the impression that you are a witness who will not be shaken if the case ever goes to trial.

Be natural, but firmly maintain your self-control.

For example, I recently defended a case involving claims for intentional and negligent infliction of emotional distress. The plaintiff claimed that the defendant (a theater owner) had caused great emotional trauma by refusing to provide a telephone when the plaintiff received word to call home because one of his children was injured. When the plaintiff was tested during the examination before trial, it became obvious that he had a severe emotional problem that had nothing to do with my client. I started the questioning using the overly nice approach, and the simplest questions caused the plaintiff to lose control of his emotions. It appeared that he was the type of person who could become emotionally upset on a daily basis, no matter what the situation.

When the case came up for trial, I knew the plaintiff's emotional propensities, and so treated him with kid gloves. It was my hope that he would display the same lack of emotional self-control in front of the jury. Sure enough, although I proceeded at a slow, almost-boring pace, without being condescending or in any way antagonistic, the plaintiff became emotionally upset on the witness stand.

After the case was thrown out, I talked to several of the jurors who told me that they thought the plaintiff was a little nuts. It was their opinion that the plaintiff would have been emotionally distressed no matter what my client had done. On that basis, they weren't going to award the plaintiff anything.

If the plaintiff hadn't demonstrated his emotional tendencies at the deposition, I would not have known his propensity for losing control. I would not have been able to plan my cross-examination in advance so that he would trip himself up at trial. I might have proceeded to question him in front of the judge and jury in a more severe manner. If I had, I might have created sympathy for the plaintiff in the eyes of the court. The jurors might have thought he was getting upset because I was picking on him. The overall result could have been very different.

SKIPPING SUBJECTS

You should be aware of another style of questioning. Lawyers sometimes have a habit of skipping around from one subject to another.

They will have you answer a question, and then go to a completely different subject, just to see if the details change at all when they come back to the original topic. This is one of the most effective ways to find out if a witness is telling the truth. If the witness makes up an answer, chances are it won't be remembered exactly when the subject is brought up again half an hour later. The witness will have been engrossed in testifying about other minute details, and the questioner will be waiting to see if the witness becomes confused and gives inconsistent testimony.

The best advice on how to deal with an attorney who is skipping around from subject to subject is simply to tell the truth. If you tell the truth, you won't have to worry about being consistent.

A deposition presents a special opportunity for the lawyer to play these kinds of games to test the witness and to get the witness to give mistaken answers. The written transcript will not indicate the tone of voice the lawyer used when asking the questions. It won't show whether the questions were rapid fire or relaxed. The transcript doesn't show whether the lawyer had glaring eyes or a broad smile, or whether he was kidding, using innuendo, or scornful. The attorney can't play these kinds of games at the actual trial, because the judge and jury will be present. But an attorney who has the witness's number before the trial starts can plan an attack carefully for trial time.

Attorneys test the truth by skipping around during questioning to see if you remember what you said.

20

THE DEFENSIVE
GAME PLAN

You will probably have a lawyer present at the examination before trial to represent you. Even independent witnesses often hire a lawyer to accompany them to a deposition. Although we refer to these lawyers as *defending* the witness, that is somewhat of a misnomer. The attorney may not be there to defend the witness as much as to supervise the proceedings so that things don't get out of hand.

For example, a few years ago I attended a deposition of a doctor in Toronto. The doctor was being deposed as an independent witness because she had treated a plaintiff who was involved in a lawsuit in New York. The doctor would not come to New York for the trial, so the attorneys went to Toronto to take her deposition. Even though the doctor wasn't being sued, she hired a lawyer to attend the deposition. The lawyer who accompanied the doctor was very careful not to allow his client to testify about anything that could later be interpreted as improper or questionable medical treatment. Even if you are not a party to the lawsuit, a legal expert can be very handy to watch out for your best interests.

Just as attorneys adopt different strategies for questioning witnesses, they also adopt different styles of representing or defending their own witnesses. Much of the defensive strategy has to do with assessing the witness before the deposition begins. If possible, the attorney will have had the time to interview the witness, and perhaps have had a practice question and answer session. If, after getting to know the witness a little, the attorney decides that the witness is not capable of testifying independently, the attorney will probably take a more active role in the deposition session.

If a lawyer feels that a witness is easily mixed up, objections will likely be raised to repetitive questions. An attempt may also be made to correct the ongoing testimony when the witness appears confused.

The defending lawyer may even ask the client some questions during the deposition if, after the other lawyers have finished their questioning, additional testimony is needed to clarify the record. At other times, an attorney who thinks the witness is getting rattled or about to make a mistake may make a series of objections to break the opponent's rhythm and give the witness a chance to regather composure. Most defending lawyers do not like to take too active a role; however, the style of defense that is used will differ with the circumstances of each case and the abilities of each witness.

I recall a story another attorney told me concerning his early training in litigation. He attended a deposition along with one of the senior attorneys from his firm, and was allowed to conduct his first deposition with his mentor watching. He felt it was his duty, as a nouveau defense attorney, to make objections whenever possible, and felt he had to thoroughly guide his client through the testimony. He threw in a few insults at opposing counsel, and gave the opposition a very rough time as the deposition continued for several hours in a fairly simple case.

He objected to the form of many of the questions that were asked, and insisted that several questions be clarified. He even tried to reword some of the opponent's questions. He felt he was doing a good job for his client. He knew he had a good case, and thought he was showing the opposition that he wasn't afraid to litigate to the max.

Finally, the senior partner asked to take a break, and took the young associate out into the hall for a discussion. My friend thought it was to discuss the case, but instead, the older attorney spent a considerable length of time criticizing the manner in which the deposition was being conducted.

He complained that the deposition would have been a lot shorter if there weren't so many objections. He went on to state that the objections being raised were valid, but meaningless. Many of the objections were made on minor and irrelevant points that would not have mattered at all in court. He then went on to explain that taking such an active role in defending the witness was probably giving the exact opposite impression from what the client would want to convey. The more objections that were made, the more the opposition was likely to think the attorney was trying to help the witness hide information.

In an effort to determine whether there were certain areas of hidden information, the opposition attorneys had started to ask every picayune question they could think of. After the hallway conference, my friend went back into the deposition room, kept his mouth shut, and finished the deposition in a matter of minutes.

The lesson to be learned from all of this is that your attorney may have a good reason to sit silently by and allow minor infractions of the rules to pass. This may be done on purpose to suggest that you are not afraid of anything the other side may ask. It also helps to shorten the examination before trial and ease some of the pressure on you.

By letting a witness stand alone, the defending attorney conveys the impression of having faith in the witness. The witness is also able to make a much better impression when fielding questions in an uninterrupted manner, without mothering or hand holding from an attorney.

Of course, the style of defense will also be based upon the overall impression that the lawyer wants the witness to make. If the witness is supposed to appear sympathetic, such as an elderly person or an injured child, the defending attorney is more likely to take an active role. The lawyer may adopt a sympathetic tone of voice, and use occasional words of encouragement to assist the witness in testifying. When conducting a deposition, the lawyer defending the witness is not just trying to assure that a proper impression is made on the record. The lawyer is also trying to help the client plant an impression in the minds of the opposition.

Whether your attorney takes an active role and raises frequent objections may depend on the circumstances of the litigation.

21

THE TRUTH, AND
NOTHING BUT THE TRUTH

I never give them hell. I just tell the truth, and
they think it is hell.

Harry S. Truman

The best advice your attorney can give you is to tell the truth. One falsehood has the potential to destroy an entire case. Lawyers love to use the argument that a witness who has lied once is probably lying about other things, and therefore shouldn't be believed at all.

A witness who cooks up stories is liable to lose credibility. A witness who tells a fib is a sitting duck. The truth holds up under cross-examination. Falsehoods usually don't.

BODY LANGUAGE

Most people have the inherent ability to tell when someone is lying. Psychologists tell us that liars exhibit certain telltale signs that give them away. Emotions are exhibited through behavior triggered by the subconscious mind. What comes out of the mouth of a liar is often contradicted by expressions in the face or movement of the shoulders, neck, and body. These movements tip us off to what is going on in the witness's mind. We pick up on these movements in much the same way as a lie detector machine is able to pick up on the reflex changes in the nervous system.

The judge's or jury's ability to spot a witness who is giving untrustworthy testimony is the basis upon which our trial system works. Juries know instinctively whether or not to believe what they hear, because they are able to observe the witness speaking. It's not hard to spot a liar in everyday conversation. It is even easier to spot a liar who tries to get away with it in a high pressure situation, such as when giving sworn testimony. The pressure intensifies because follow-up questions can be used to see if the lie will hold up.

Fabricating testimony is dangerous, because your body language may give you away.

Lawyers are experts at spotting and discrediting dishonest witnesses. They look for indicators that cannot be controlled by the conscious mind, such as witnesses who blush, whose facial muscles twitch, who shift in their seats uncontrollably, who break out in a cold sweat, exhibit a change in tone of voice, fidget, swallow too often, appear overly nervous, or fail to look the questioner squarely in the eyes.

LANGUAGE

Lawyers are also trained to carefully scrutinize the words that are spoken. Important details that are missing, or wording that sounds too pat or flat, is a sure giveaway that the witness is being less than truthful.

If your wording sounds too slick, you may give away a lack of truthfulness.

The more dishonest witnesses an attorney has to deal with over time, the more expert that attorney becomes in spotting falsehoods and dealing with them. A trial attorney soon learns how to set a trap for the fibber. This becomes especially easy when lying witnesses feel compelled to over-explain, as if trying to convince themselves of the validity of their own answers.

DIGGING THE HOLE

The interrogator who intends to destroy the credibility of the witness will rarely confront the lie immediately. Instead, the lawyer will play along, acting as if the testimony is believable, and allowing the witness to build lie upon lie until it all comes crashing down with one very pointed and revealing series of questions.

Confronting the witness immediately might force more truthful answers, or provide the opportunity for the witness to cover up. So, instead, the interrogator will let small untruths and exaggerations go by until a pattern of untruths and exaggeration in the witness's testimony can be established. Meanwhile, the witness may think he's getting away with it, and, by the time he finds out he's not getting away with anything, it's too late. Credibility has already been lost, and the case may be lost as well.

Attorneys will probe small untruths and exaggerations as the deposition proceeds.

CREDIBILITY

Perhaps the second most important piece of advice your attorney can give you is to not be afraid of the truth. What may appear to be a harmful fact may turn out to be useful if looked at from the right perspective. It may also be helpful to remember that deposition testimony becomes a written record that can be used in cases other than the one being litigated when the testimony occurs. It would be very unfortunate if you hedged on the truth only to find that the statements come back to haunt you in another proceeding.

Every lawsuit involves a multitude of details that tend to distract from the ability to concentrate on the big picture. The overall meshing together of the facts is what counts. One hurtful truth can be offset by dozens of helpful truths as the details of the case are examined. But nothing offsets an obvious lie. It is well-known that judges and juries are sympathetic to human foibles. They are, however, extremely unforgiving if they think you are purposely lying to them.

The possibility of losing credibility should be enough to encourage any witness to tell the truth. In case it isn't, our legal system has provided the witness with further incentive. Lying under oath has been made a crime.

Your honest approach to what appears to be damaging testimony may give you the increased credibility needed to win your case.

PERJURY

A witness who willfully gives a false answer while under oath (or otherwise qualified) at an examination before trial is guilty of *perjury*. Perjury is considered a serious crime. To insure that witnesses are not tempted to perjure themselves, our system imposes stiff fines, and in some cases jail terms, when perjury is committed. What starts out as merely a civil lawsuit may have criminal consequences if a witness tries to tell a lie under oath.

Having said all of that, it is interesting to note two things about our legal system's requirements for true testimony given under oath. One is that there is a semantic difference between telling the "truth" and telling the "whole truth." The second is that the oath does not apply to everyone at the deposition (e.g., to the lawyers).

You are probably familiar with the oath that recites "the truth, the whole truth, and nothing but the truth." In reality, it is rare, if ever, that the whole truth comes out during the course of a lawsuit. This is because, although sworn to tell the whole truth, a witness is in practice not required to volunteer information. It is not perjury to simply respond to a question and say no more, even though you know the question could have been phrased to require more important details.

Perjury is a serious crime and you must not knowingly make a false statement, but don't volunteer additional information.

In addition, the oath to tell the whole truth only applies to the person who takes it. The attorneys don't take the oath, and, as Professor Alan Dershowitz has pointed out, "they couldn't. Indeed, it is fair to say that the American justice system is built on the foundation of NOT telling the whole truth." Rarely does a lawyer actually want the whole truth to come out.

As an advocate for one side of a controversy, the lawyer is allowed to conduct the case and present the evidence in the light most favorable to the client. That means the other side must ask the right questions to get at the whole truth, and there is no requirement that a witness voluntarily lay the information at the adversary's feet.

22

TAKING THE FIFTH

Under the fifth and fourteenth amendments to the United States Constitution, you have the right to refuse to give evidence that may be self-incriminating in state or federal courts. This means that you may refuse to answer any question in a civil proceeding if the answer may be used against you in a criminal proceeding.

Self-incrimination situations don't arise very often during a civil deposition. Attorneys usually try to wait until any pending criminal action is resolved before proceeding with a corresponding civil action. This is because the results of the criminal action can often be used as a bargaining chip for settlement of the civil claim. The witness who refuses to answer because of a pending criminal action may have to appear at a further deposition to answer the question once the criminal action has been resolved.

If you are an independent witness, and you even slightly suspect the possibility that something potentially incriminating will come up at an examination before trial, make sure that you have your own attorney present to represent your interests. You should not merely rely on your own judgment in deciding whether to answer a potentially incriminating question. Technical legal advice may be required.

For example, if the time limitations in the criminal matter have run out, or if the underlying criminal action is only a misdemeanor, you may still have to answer the question. However, if the answer could be used to prosecute you under a conspiracy charge, and the statutory time limit has not run out on that aspect of prosecution, you probably won't have to answer.

Although you have the right to take the fifth and refuse to answer self-incriminating questions, seek legal counsel to be sure your objection is valid.

Having legal counsel readily available is important because once you give an answer, you may have waived any right you have against self-incrimination. The damage could be irreparable.

CONSULTING DURING THE EBT

During the course of the deposition, you are free to take a break and privately discuss a potential answer with your attorney. You may take as many breaks as you desire, unless the breaks are being taken only to disrupt the proceedings. If you are being disruptive, the attorneys may apply to the court to make you more cooperative.

You are permitted to consult privately with your attorney during the deposition, but this may reflect poorly on your answers. Do not use this to be disruptive.

You should also remember that, each time a break is taken, the transcript will show that there was an interruption in the proceedings. A smart opposing attorney will develop the record to show what happened when the break was taken. Later, at trial, you may be forced to admit that there was a private conversation with your attorney before you answered.

It is not a good idea to claim the fifth amendment privilege just to avoid answering an embarrassing question. When the case later comes up for trial, the opposing attorney may comment to the jury about any questions you refused to answer, thereby planting negative inferences in the minds of the jurors. The judge and jury will draw an assumption about why you didn't want to answer, which can be damaging to the case and your credibility. Moreover, if your refusal to answer turns out to be groundless, it can lead to a contempt of court proceeding, resulting in stiff fines or imprisonment.

The best course to take is to use the available opportunity to consult with your attorney, and not to exercise the fifth amendment privilege unless it is really necessary.

23

NEVER, NEVER, NEVER VOLUNTEER

Think all you speak, but speak not all you
think. Thoughts are your own but [spoken]
words are so no more.

Delany

It is up to the attorney asking the questions to ask the right questions. It is up to the attorney asking the questions to make a case on the record. If the attorney doesn't ask the right questions, don't help out. It's not your responsibility to help the other side prepare its case.

The best witness is the one who will listen carefully to the question, answer only the question that is being asked, answer in as few words as possible, and then shut up!

RESPONDING TO QUESTIONS

A favorite ploy used by some attorneys is to create what is referred to as the "uncomfortable silence." After the witness responds, the lawyer will look at the witness as if to imply that the answer was not complete. The lawyer may even say "go on," creating in the witness a feeling that further elaboration is required. It isn't. If your answer was complete, you should just sit silently and wait for the next question.

Concentrate on what you are being asked and only answer that much.

The deposition is not the place to try to prove your side of the story. You are not there to volunteer any information, only to respond to proper questions. If you are a party to the lawsuit, you are called to the deposition because the opposing party wants to ask you questions. The more you say, the more follow-up questions you will be asked.

Responding to the questions requires some concentration. Not only do you have to listen carefully to each question, you must also try to answer only the question that is asked. Notice how the following witness digs a hole for himself by failing to stick to just answering the question he is asked:

Q. What makes you think they were intoxicated?

A. Because I myself was pretty straight. I don't drink that much. When we go to Sam's Bar, we go there to have a good time. I know three quarters of the people that work there. So, all we're doing is, you know, chew the beef, you know, shooting the bull. That's about it. We ain't doing no drinking.

DEFENDANT'S ATTORNEY: That wasn't his question though.

EXAMINING ATTORNEY: My question is, how did you know—you claimed earlier that Mr. Essjay and Mr. Farberlake were intoxicated.

THE WITNESS: I walked up, like I was telling you. I could smell it on them, plus the way they were acting.

Q. How were they acting?

A. Very uptight, you know. They were mad. They were mad.

Q. Okay.

A. Upset.

Q. How were you acting?

A. I was mellow.

Q. You were mellow? You were mellow?

A. Yeah.

Q. How was Mr. Sheridan acting?

A. Mellow, very severely. It was like a flash. It just happened like that, boom, it was over with.

Q. So, you were the only mellow guys there, and everybody else was upset?

DEFENDANT'S ATTORNEY: I object to the form of the question.

THE WITNESS: My mellow and your mellow are two different mellows.

Q. Must be. I guess the reason I asked you that question is because I just—I find it hard to believe.

A. Calm, that's the word I would use.

Q. You were the only calm guys there? They got hit from behind. You claim they were intoxicated because they were upset?

DEFENDANT'S ATTORNEY: I object to the form of the question.

THE WITNESS: They were slurring their words.

EXAMINING ATTORNEY: Have you ever worked as a police officer anywhere?

THE WITNESS: Is this a joke?

Q. No, seriously, have you ever worked as a police officer?

A. No.

Q. Have you ever worked in a DWI program?

A. No way.

Q. Have you ever worked in a drug or an alcohol abuse program?

A. Never.

Q. Do you have any experience at all in identifying anyone who's—had any professional experience in identifying people who have taken drugs or alcohol?

A. Yeah, I could.

Q. How so, what's your professional experience?

A. Well, I would—I myself would do like a cop would do. Make you walk a straight line.

Q. Did anyone ever pay you to do it?

A. No.

Q. Then you have no professional experience, do you?

A. Not at all.

Q. Your only experience then would be only—only your personal knowledge?

A. I know when somebody is drunk, put it that way.

Q. You know that how?

A. By looking at them, listening to them.

Q. How did you learn that?

A. By going to bars and watching people get drunk.

Q. And you've stated that you go to bars a lot, or this Sam's Bar anyway, and you watch people get drunk a lot?

A. Oh yeah.

Q. You ever get drunk yourself?

A. Yeah, lots of times.

A sharp lawyer can take volunteered information and twist it around to make the witness change the underlying meaning of the testimony. The witness quoted above was initially asked a simple question about how he knew somebody had been drinking. He obviously made certain observations, and stated, "I could smell it," and "They were slurring their words." He could tell they were drunk by "looking at them and listening to them." When asked the question, he should have stated these observations and nothing more.

This kind of witness is every lawyer's nightmare (except the opposition's). Instead of listening to the questions and carefully responding, he handed the opposition the axe with which to chop his testimony to bits. The witness voluntarily admitted: (1) that he knew three-quarters of the people who worked at Sam's Bar; (2) that the incident was over in a flash; (3) that he knows how police officers give sobriety tests; and (4) that he has lots of experience going to bars, watching people get drunk, and getting drunk himself. Most jurors would conclude from this information that the witness was a habitual drinker, if not a habitual bar brawler. Notice that the attorney also lead this witness to substantially contradict his earlier statement when he said, "I don't drink that much." Notice also that this witness volunteered all of this information without ever being asked one pertinent question on the subjects that ultimately submarined his credibility. If he had stuck to only answering the questions he was asked, he probably would have been able to state his observations without calling into question his own trustworthiness.

EXTRA COMMENTS

Avoid extra comments—be direct.

There are other ways that witnesses frequently volunteer information without intending to. One of these is to make comments instead of giving direct answers:

Q. So, in your view, as the engineer in charge of safety, the curb barrier was enough to insure the safety of the traveling public?

A. That combined with the upright barrier.

Q. All right. How about past the upright barrier, where there was a ditch that started—where there was a 20 inch ditch. Did you consider that safe for the traveling public?
A. A lot of cars went in there, no one got injured.
Q. A lot of cars went in there?
A. Yes.
Q. And no one got injured?
A. Not that I know of.
Q. Well, did it occur to you that—as the engineer in charge of safety, did it occur to you that if a lot of cars went in there, some day someone was going to get very injured?
A. No.
Q. And you were the person who was in charge of the safety of the traveling public, but you didn't think of it?
A. No.

The witness was asked whether, in his opinion, the area was safe. He obviously thought it was. He should have just said so. Instead, he chose to make a comment. This information was extremely damaging to his side's case, because he volunteered that he knew lots of cars were going into the ditch. So much for his expert opinion that the road was safe!

ADDING WORDS

Another way to accidentally volunteer information is to simply add an unnecessary word. One or two poorly chosen words thrown into an answer can be thrown right back in your face:

Choose your words carefully and use as few as possible. Don't try to tell a story, just answer.

Q. Have you been involved in any accident or had any subsequent injuries we should know about, since this accident we're talking about?
A. No. Oh, yes, I did.
Q. How did this happen?
A. I fell on a bag of money. I mean I slipped and fell, and I landed on a bag of money.
Q. How much money?
A. I think I had about three thousand dollars in the two bags.

Q. And you were carrying these bags of money around when
   you fell and were injured?
PLAINTIFF'S ATTORNEY: Is this really relevant?

What was the witness's purpose in telling the part about the bags
of money? Wouldn't it have been better for the witness to merely say
she slipped and fell? A smart lawyer might take that testimony and keep
repeating the words "bags of money" at trial to make it sound like the
witness, Miss Money Bags, is trying to fall into money again by bringing
a lawsuit. Other inferences can also be made with this information. If
this person was injured, what was she doing carrying around bags full
of cash? The opposing lawyer knows the jury is less likely to feel sympathy for someone who has lots of money to carry around. If the witness hadn't voluntarily mentioned the subject of money bags, it probably would never have come out.

If you are called upon to testify at an EBT, you are in a position
similar to a goalie at a soccer or hockey game. Your best bet is to concentrate on handling the shots from the opposition. You should not try
to play an offensive game at the same time. If you try to score a point
or two against the other side, you take chances and leave yourself
open, making it easier for the other side to score against you. To be a
good deposition witness, always play it close to the net.

24

MAKING THE RECORD

Entering the deposition room is like entering upon a stage. Your aim is to give your best performance, and there are certain contingencies to avoid because they may affect the presentation.

REMEMBER THE RECORD

To be a skillfull deponent, you must keep the ultimate objective of the deposition, the record that is being made, in the back of your mind at all times. Because it may be used as evidence, or to cross-examine at trial, the record is extremely important.

Try to visualize what the testimony will look like when it is typed in transcript form. Each word that appears should have a purpose. Your testimony should be clear and concise. Don't think out loud. To be an effective witness, think to yourself before uttering the words.

Before you speak, picture how your words will appear on the record.

Hesitancy in a witness's voice and rising inflections in speech do not show up on the printed transcript. What shows up instead is a sentence that, although not originally uttered with certainty, appears to have been an emphatic statement:

Q. Mr. Johnson would have been in charge of Mr. Morris?
A. Mr. Morris was directly in charge of our foreman, and Mr. Johnson is Mr. Morris' superior.
Q. Is he still employed with American Strongwood?
A. Mr. Johnson?

Q. Yes.

A. Yes, sir.

Q. What title does he have with the company?

A. Supervisor of Timber Procurement.

WITNESS'S ATTORNEY: Are you sure of that? You don't sound
sure.

THE WITNESS: I'm not sure of that, no, I don't know what his
title was at the time.

The above is an example of a witness who was thinking out loud and guessing when he testified. When he said the words "Supervisor of Timber Procurement," he said them with a rise in his voice as if he were actually asking a question. However, if you examine the transcript, what actually appears in print looks like he was stating a fact.

In this particular situation, the attorney defending the witness interrupted to clarify the record. He asked his own witness a question to show that the words spoken by the deponent were not to be taken as a statement of fact in the record. In the previous example, the witness almost misstated the authority of Mr. Johnson to enter into the contract that was the subject of the lawsuit. If the attorney had not been thinking in terms of what the record would look like, the testimony would have contained what appeared to be incorrect information. If the attorney had not chimed in to clarify the record, the witness might have been stuck with a situation in which his mere thoughts could be interpreted as a declaration of fact. A jury, to whom the transcript was read, might think the witness was a liar, or at least that he incorrectly asserted as the truth things he knew very little about.

Unfortunately, you can't depend on your attorney to catch every instance where your manner of speech might be inaccurately reflected in the printed words of the transcript. The best way to avoid this problem is to think before speaking, and to try to form the response in a manner that is complete and declarative.

IF YOU MAKE A MISTAKE

"Making the record" also means making the record correct. Just about everyone will make some sort of mistake when testifying. Major mistakes should not be allowed to pass by without correction.

Witnesses will often give answers that they think are correct, only to realize later, while answering another question, that the earlier answer was, in fact, incorrect. If this happens, you should immediately stop everything and correct the previous testimony.

If you realize you've made a mistake, stop and correct it on the record.

The proper way to do so is to say, "Excuse me, I want to go back to something I said before. I think I said . . . I should have said. . . ." This will prevent the opposing attorney from using the incorrect answer for impeachment (contradiction) purposes at trial. You could merely point out to the court that the mistake was corrected a few pages later in the transcript.

REMEMBER YOUR PURPOSE

Finally, when you consider making the record, you should also consider that one of the purposes of the transcript is to preserve the testimony to be used at trial. Every witness has a purpose, and it is likely that each witness will have certain information that, out of necessity, should be placed on the record in the correct form. Keep this in mind, and be prepared to speak the appropriate words to accomplish the underlying purpose of your testimony.

Keep your overall purpose in mind as you speak.

For instance, in order for an expert's testimony to be admissible at trial, the expert must be able to state an opinion with a reasonable degree of certainty. It may be necessary for a scientist to make statements "with scientific probability," or for a doctor to state an impression "with a reasonable degree of medical certainty," in order for the record to be admissible. An attorney can advise the witness of the appropriate technical prerequisites.

The simplest testimony and responses to the most basic questions may be supremely important when considered as part of the overall lawsuit. Something as basic as telling a little about your personal background can have the greatest consequences. Answers to seemingly insignificant questions may form the legally required foundation for your qualifications to give answers to other questions.

After the deposition is over, it may be too late to go back and modify the record. Keeping in mind that the ultimate purpose of the testimony is to make a record will help you to focus on what is happening while you are testifying, and will help you to accomplish making the record you intend to make.

25

THE SUPREMES
AND THE TEMPTATIONS

The supreme answer is usually a short, declarative sentence. The best answer you can give, where appropriate, is a simple, declarative "yes" or "no." If the question can't be answered in that way, stick to using as few words as possible. The more you say, the more follow-up questions you will have to deal with.

    If you want to give the supreme answers, you must try to avoid the following usual temptations.

Short declarative answers are best.

THE TEMPTATION TO BE FACETIOUS

Don't be flippant. You may know that your statement was made in a jesting manner, but the levity in your voice won't be show up on the printed transcript.

Remember, your tone of voice doesn't show up in the written transcript.

> Q. These were the installation instructions?
> A. The installation instruction sheet would be for what is known as the Ajax Ensign, E-N-S-I-G-N.
> Q. Is that a marketing name?
> A. Yes.
> Q. To the best of your knowledge, sir, have there been any changes in the design of that machine from 1987 to today?

A. Under that name, no. There is a new model that has super-
seded this entire design about 1986, and it became known
as the New Ensign. A major, sweeping change.

When this witness said the words "a major, sweeping change," he
thought he was being funny. He was facetiously telling the lawyers at
the deposition that the major change in the design was that they
changed the name from the "Ensign" to the "New Ensign." His tone of
voice is not reproduced in the written record. His facetious remark is
now embodied in the text as testimony that the company made major,
sweeping changes in the design, which is exactly the opposite of what
he intended to say.

Testifying at an examination before trial is different from testifying
before a judge and jury. In open court, there is the opportunity to
observe the witness and hear the tone of voice. A remark that is
intended to be humorous may lose its humorous context and become
completely inappropriate when translated into the cold, hard print of a
deposition transcript.

THE TEMPTATION TO BE EVASIVE

Being evasive is usually a poor strategy.

Every deposition will involve certain questions that are embarrassing or
hurtful to your case. Trying to evade them is not wise. It will be even
more embarrassing and hurtful to your case if you appear to be a witness who is trying to weasel out of giving an obvious answer:

Q. Sir, as you're sitting here today, do you realize there are
consequences for sending in an improper, negative credit
rating on somebody?

A. I wasn't aware of any, no.

Q. What—what did you think would happen to Bunkport
Corporation's credit rating when you sent in a negative
credit report? What did you expect to happen?

A. I didn't expect anything to happen.

Q. Did you have any conception that it might affect Mr.
Kenney or his business, with respect to his credit rating for
example?

A. No.

Q. So, your testimony here today is that you had no idea that your sending in a negative credit rating on somebody's business would have any effect whatsoever? Is that your testimony?

A. It may have an effect. I don't know.

Q. Why did you send this in? Why did you send it?

A. We send it in every month.

Q. Well, why? Why did you send it in on this particular company? Why did you send it in?

A. It's a service of the credit reporting agency that we can use.

Q. Well, why did you send it in? I mean, I—I know it's a service, but why did you use it? Why did you report this? What were your reasons, what were your thoughts? If you didn't have any reason at all, then tell me that. I want to know what your thinking process was. You authorized it to be sent in. I want to know what was your thinking?

A. I wasn't thinking anything, other than we had had a bad experience and it was a report.

Q. What did you think would be done with the report once you sent it in?

A. I don't know what they do with it.

Q. You don't know what they do with it? Had you ever had a bad credit report sent in on your company or you?

A. I don't know.

Q. Do you know what the purpose of this service is? Do you know what the purpose of a credit reporting service is?

A. Somebody can call up and find out if a certain company has good credit or not.

Q. All right, and if somebody called up and found that there was a complaint or report of bad credit, do you think that would adversely affect the business of the company that had the bad report?

A. I don't know. I suppose it could.

This witness did not do himself any favors. The answers were obvious. Nevertheless, he refused to testify in an open and direct manner. He gave the impression that he was foolish enough to think he could play dumb and get away with it. A jury might conclude from this testimony that the witness was a liar and that any other testimony he gave was equally unreliable. A more sympathetic reading of this testimony suggests this witness may have had some personal doubts about his own conduct, and that he may have felt somewhat guilty.

THE TEMPTATION TO MAKE COMMENTS

Because every word you say will become part of the record, avoid the temptation to say anything other than direct answers to the questions you are asked:

> Q. You understand that my name is Michael Terrier and I represent your brother, Mr. Churchmouse.
> A. Yes, I'm sorry about that.
> Q. Sorry that I represent your brother, or sorry that you just kicked me under the table?

It is easy to see how a simple comment, like "I'm sorry," could become embodied in the record without an explanation. What if the witness had made the "I'm sorry" comment at some other point in the testimony, and there was no explanation given? It might be read back to the jury like this:

> Q. You employed the wrong chemical compound in this particular batch of the formula—
> A. I'm sorry about that.
> Q. —and it lowered the flash point and increased the combustability, making the solution more hazardous to the user?
> A. I don't know.

Avoid editorial comments and unnecessary speech.

Every word you, as witness, say will be taken down by the court reporter. What you may think is just an off-hand comment can acquire dramatic meaning when embodied in the transcript. The only way to be sure an unnecessary comment doesn't make its way into the record is to avoid making such comments altogether.

THE TEMPTATION TO GO "OFF THE RECORD"

Witnesses sometimes think that they can clear up issues by making comments "off the record." While there are occasions on which the lawyers will conduct off the record discussions and the reporter will be instructed to stop taking notes, a witness cannot ask the reporter to stop. Even if you get the lawyers to agree that the reporter should stop recording the testimony temporarily while you make an off-record comment, any one of the lawyers can ask you to repeat the comment on the record.

The lawyers decide whether any talking can take place off the record.

THE TEMPTATION TO MAKE SPEECHES

Keep your answers short. Avoid the temptation to elaborate. You're not at the deposition to give a discourse on the subject of the litigation or any other subject. Say only the words necessary to give a direct answer to the question. Then stop talking! The more you say, the more you are likely to accidentally help your opponent.

> Q. What kinds of problems do you have in the winter from the ribs?
> A. Just kind of like a pleurisy, like a pain, like you got a cold.
> Q. How often do you get that?
> A. If I go out and stand in the cold weather too long.
> Q. Do you shovel your driveway?
> A. No.
> Q. Use a snow blower?
> A. No.
> Q. Do you have a plowing service?
> A. The Lord put it there, the Lord takes it away. I haven't shoveled a driveway in thirty years. You just don't go to work, that's all.
> Q. What's that?
> A. I say, if it gets too deep, you don't go to work, that's all, that's the way I feel about it. If it snows, don't go to work.
> Q. So, in other words, although you are claiming that you lost time from work, on any of those days that it snowed, you wouldn't have gone to work anyway?

Along the same lines, resist the temptation to make excuses and explanations. If you are not asked for this information at the examination before trial, don't worry. The explanation may still be used effectively in the courtroom.

The more you say, the more potential there is to accidently help your opponent.

It may be to your strategic benefit not to give away your explanation at the time of the deposition. It may also be an explanation that sounds good to you, but comes out horribly when not prepared and phrased properly.

One last time: Stick to giving short answers whenever possible.

26

YES OR NO

Perhaps 90 percent of all questions asked at a deposition can be answered with "yes," "no," "I don't know," or "I don't remember." You should, of course, be careful not to say "yes" or "no" to a question that you can't truthfully answer in that way, but you should not be afraid to answer yes or no whenever possible.

Most properly worded questions can be answered with a simple "yes" or "no."

Don't try to qualify or explain your answer. If the question involves some detail that prevents you from saying yes or no, use your judgment to decide whether the detail is significant. If not, even though you may feel the answer is damaging to your case, just say yes or no and leave it at that for now.

A good witness pays attention to detail, but a good witness is not necessarily a stickler for literalness. For example, if a witness is asked, "At the meeting, did any money change hands?" and the witness knows that cash was not used but that a check was, how does the witness properly answer the question?

If the question is taken literally, it would be permissible to say no. Money did not change hands. But to answer "no" would be misleading, because the witness knows that a payment was actually made. In addition, if the witness answers "no," there is the possibility that the opposition has enough knowledge of the situation to probe further with follow-up questions. When the truth comes out, the witness will look foolish, or appear to have been intentionally and dishonestly trying to hide the information.

The best way to handle this kind of situation might be to answer, "Not money, but a check was exchanged." If the detail of whether it was cash or a check is not important to the case, the best answer would probably be to simply say "yes."

Not only is the shorter answer usually a better and more direct answer, but it helps to shorten the examination before trial. In the previous example, several minutes are cut by not forcing the opposition to probe for the unimportant details. Usually, there is little to be gained by prolonging a deposition or answering in an obstructive manner.

27

I Don't Know/
I Can't
Remember

We're all trained in this grade school routine. From our early childhood educational experience, we become used to the idea that when someone asks a question, we're supposed to be able to provide an answer. In school, if we didn't know an answer, chances are we at least tried to guess. We were taught to learn from our mistakes. If we were wrong, the teacher merely went on to some other student to make the correction. This predisposition to give answers causes most deposition witnesses to stretch and strain to try to provide information that may not exist. An examination under oath is no place to start guessing.

As a deposition witness, you are called upon to testify about your own knowledge. That means you testify only about what you know and what you remember. If the answer is something you should know, but you draw a blank, there is nothing wrong with saying "I don't know" or "I don't remember." If you suddenly remember the information later during the deposition, you can ask for the opportunity to change your previous testimony.

No one is really expected to remember every detail. In fact, in some cases, remembering too much may appear suspicious. Everyone has different memory powers. You should not be afraid to be yourself and admit when your memory fails.

NOBODY KNOWS IT ALL

If you don't know the answer or can't remember it, say so—don't guess.

Sometimes it is a matter of professional pride. A witness can find it hard to resist showing off expertise and may state something assuming it is correct, while, in fact, having no knowledge or memory on the subject. It is also foolish to volunteer answers like "It might have happened," or "Maybe it happened," since these types of answers sound more like the witness is trying to cover up than be truthful. A simple, honest "I don't remember" would be better.

It is a sad state of affairs when a witness testifies to something under oath and then realizes on the way home that the information was incorrect. Having to make some sort of delayed explanation for the testimony, such as trying to correct the transcript or delivering an explanation at trial, presents a real predicament. The correction always sounds suspicious because it is offered in the form of an excuse.

It is possible to preface your answers by saying, "I'm not sure, but I think. . . ." However, this is also a dangerous practice. You may end up volunteering information unwittingly, or you may be asked to explain why you "think" that's the answer.

Another common error is in trying to explain why you don't know something or why you can't remember:

Q. And was it still raining at the time?

A. Yes, I think so, I'm not sure.

Q. Were there any other cars traveling in the same direction as you, either behind you or in front of you?

A. I don't know because I really wasn't paying attention.

Q. Were there cars coming in the opposite direction?

A. I don't recall whether there were cars going in either direction.

Q. So is it fair to say that you weren't paying attention to other cars in any direction?

A. No, I said I don't remember.

Q. The record will also reflect that you said you don't remember about the cars in front of you because you weren't paying any attention.

A. I don't think that's what I said.

There was no need for this witness to admit he "really wasn't pay-ing attention." A simple "I don't recall" would have been sufficient. This witness has provided his opponents with an opportunity for effective cross-examination at trial. The opposing attorney, deposition transcript in hand, will now be able to ask, "Isn't it true that you don't recall the location of the other vehicles on the road because you weren't paying attention?" If the witness tries to claim otherwise, the attorney will merely quote the answer verbatim from the transcript.

You should not only be careful to avoid making excuses for failing to remember details, but likewise you should not offer justification for remembering certain details. Saying something like, "I remember that clearly because it was the day after my birthday," serves no real pur-pose. Such comments are also potentially dangerous because you may be volunteering information that wasn't requested. Instead of giving the questioner a reason to start asking questions about how you were out celebrating your birthday the night before the incident, just tell what you know and wait to see if the attorney is interested enough to probe the reason you remember details so well.

If you give a response like, "I can't remember," the lawyer may ask a few more questions to try to jog your memory. If the information isn't vital to the case, the questioner will probably just go on to something else. But, if you choose to answer and you are wrong, there may be dire consequences. When the case goes to trial, that inaccurate recollection may reflect badly on the truth of the important testimony, even though the inaccuracy only dealt with a minor detail, because it is a reflection on your memory. The safer route, when you don't know the answer, no matter how important or unimportant the detail, is to state your lack of knowledge or recall and leave it at that.

It is also a poor idea to try to conserve testimony by claiming that you don't remember something at the deposition, and thinking that you can testify later in court that you remembered after having a chance to reflect. You will only look foolish when questioned at trial about the fact that you knew you were going to testify at a deposition, you dis-cussed the case with a lawyer beforehand, and you pretty much knew what you were going to testify about. Of course, people do sometimes suffer memory lapses, but it is hard to convince a court that you didn't have an adequate opportunity to think about the case before testifying at the examination before trial.

AGAIN, THE TRUTH

It is perjury to say you don't know if you do—not knowing and not remembering are not the same thing.

One final word of caution: It is a violation of the oath to say "I don't know" or "I don't remember" if you really do. You are sworn to tell the truth. If you testify under oath that you don't know something when you really do know it, you are committing the crime of perjury.

In that respect, remember that there is a semantic difference between *not knowing something* and *not remembering at the moment*. Not remembering implies that you did know the answer at some point in time. Therefore, be careful not to use the two answers interchangeably.

28

HARD EVIDENCE

There are two kinds of evidence to deal with at a deposition. Testimony is one type of evidence, and the other type comprises exhibits.

In addition to testifying about your own knowledge, you often have to deal with information that exists in substantive form. This is the so-called hard evidence. Exhibits are hard because, unlike a witness, they don't have a memory that forgets over time. Hard evidence, like something written in stone, is capable of providing exactly the same information for many years.

Virtually any type of evidence that can be used in the courtroom can be discovered before trial. Consequently, the same piece of hard evidence that will be brought in for the trial may be used as an exhibit during the deposition.

Many types of hard evidence may be subjected to pretrial discovery. Items such as photographs, plans, diagrams, files full of test results, tax records, broken machine parts, cancelled checks, copies of contracts, and other documents often find their way into the deposition room.

The deposition notice, or subpoena served upon the witness, will often include a list of items the witness must bring to the deposition. Courts are very liberal in forcing production of hard evidence. Practically nothing will be treated as private.

Parties sometimes request written agreements to restrict the use of confidential materials beyond the scope of the lawsuit. But unless the court decides that it would be costly or burdensome to produce a particular item of hard evidence at the deposition, just about anything is likely to show up.

A two-step process is used at the examination before trial when a witness is questioned about a piece of hard evidence. The item must first be identified and then marked for future reference. The court reporter usually affixes a label or stamp to the item and a number or symbol is assigned such as "Exhibit A" or "Plaintiff's Exhibit #1 For Identification." The lawyer will then refer to the identification code when asking questions about the item:

Q. I show you what's been marked as Defendant's Exhibit E for identification, and ask if you can identify what's depicted in that photograph?

A. Yes, that's the McDonalds restaurant.

Q. The one that you have referred to that you visited?

A. Yes.

Q. And Exhibit F, is that also a picture—does that show the same McDonalds we're talking about?

A. It appears to, yes.

Q. Would you please take this pen and circle or mark an X on the photograph, Exhibit F, to indicate the West driveway?

A. Okay.

Q. Now would you please mark your initials next to where you marked the West driveway?

A. All right.

Q. And, sir, is that the driveway that you testified you drove into on June 13th?

A. I think it must have been.

Q. Is there a sign at the end of the driveway in that picture, Exhibit F, just above where you marked the photograph?

A. There is in this picture, yes.

Q. And that sign says what?

A. Exit Only.

Q. Exit only?

A. It does here, I mean in this photograph, isn't—I don't remember—that is I don't think that sign was there that day.

Q. You don't recall seeing the sign that appears in photograph Exhibit F marked for identification?

A. I don't recall seeing it that day, no.

This dialogue points out the cardinal rule for testifying about hard evidence. Be 100 percent sure about what you are identifying, or else indicate in your testimony that you cannot positively identify it. When the witness in this case identified the photograph of the hamburger stand, he just happened to be looking at a photo of another hamburger stand, owned by the same company, located on the same major highway, a few miles away.

The witness identifying the McPhoto probably assumed that because the layout of the hamburger stand was a crucial factor in the case, the photographer had been sent to take a few McPictures. Unfortunately, the misinformed photographer had visited the wrong location and provided the plaintiff's attorney with photographs of the other hamburger stand.

As it turned out, the witness was correct that he didn't see the "Exit Only" sign on the day in question. It turned out there was no such sign at the other location.

The witness naturally assumed that he would be shown evidence that had something to do with his lawsuit. This is a bad assumption to make. Never assume that just because you are shown some evidence by one of the lawyers it has to be the right evidence. It might be a trap. It might also be merely a McStake.

A few other simple rules will help you to deal effectively with hard evidence:

Be sure of what you're identifying when dealing with pieces of evidence.

1. Make Sure you are Referring to the Right Exhibit

Follow these six rules when exhibits are used.

Listen to the question. Be careful to look at the right item. Don't be viewing Exhibit #24 if the question is about Exhibit #23. Don't testify about any exhibit unless you have it in front of you, and you carefully consider the question being asked.

2. Make Sure it is All There

If you are asked to identify something, be sure to point out that it might be missing some pages or parts. This is not always easy to do. You may be shown a lease or contract containing 80 pages or more. Forget the fact that the other people in the room are impatiently staring at you and awaiting your answer. Take your time and be cautious about identifying the evidence. If necessary, ask for a recess in the proceedings while you review the exhibit.

3. Review the Whole Exhibit

Don't just look at one portion of the exhibit. Even if you are only being questioned on part of it, or even if your attention is being drawn to one particular aspect, it is important to be familiar with the entire item.

4. Don't Ask Questions

Don't say, "Gee, where are the margin notes I penciled in?" When you ask questions about the exhibit, you run the risk of volunteering information unnecessarily. If you can't identify an exhibit, or you can't answer a question by merely looking at it, there will surely be some follow-up questions about why you are unable to make the identification.

5. Name It

When you speak about an exhibit, be sure you adequately identify what you are talking about. If it has been marked for identification, mention the number so the record will be clear about exactly what the item was. If the item isn't marked with a code, describe it: "I'm looking at the message addressed to Mr. Jones dated July 4, 1992."

6. Don't Trust the Lawyer's Characterizations

Don't assume that the lawyer is correctly stating the contents or describing the exhibit. Check for yourself, and make corrections before you answer.

One final tip regarding hard evidence: If it's yours, make sure you eventually get it back. If you don't ask for the evidence after the litigation is over, you may never see it again. Lawyers are notoriously forgetful when they settle or finish cases. The evidence often gets filed away with the paperwork.

Sometimes, the exhibits produced and marked at an examination before trial are left with the court reporter. In the past, original documents had to be annexed to the EBT transcript. However, it is more common now to have a photocopier handy, so that one of the lawyers can keep the original exhibit and provide everyone else with a complete copy. In fact, it is a good idea to try to anticipate the items that will be used as exhibits and arrange with your lawyer to bring copies to the deposition. This will not only save time, it will enable the lawyers and the deponent to refer to copies of the same exhibits without standing around gazing over each other's shoulders.

Bring copies of the important documents to the deposition.

29

THREE RULES FOR GIVING YOUR BEST TESTIMONY

RULE 1: PAUSE BEFORE YOU SPEAK

I have made this rule number one because it is the most important habit a deposition witness can develop. Also, unless you comply with this rule, the other two rules will be practically impossible to follow.

Always pause a few seconds before you begin to answer a question. While this sounds simple, it takes some concentration to develop this technique. Witnesses (and to some extent, lawyers) have a tendency to become caught up emotionally during a deposition.

The urge to be spontaneous is involved in any series of questions and answers. This is because we grow up conducting conversations in which we respond as soon as the other person finishes—or sometimes, we interrupt and cut the question short before the other person is done.

It is important to remember that a deposition is not supposed to be a conversation. You are supposed to supply answers to oral questions, just as you would supply answers to the same questions if they were presented in written form.

To best understand the reason for pausing before you speak, consider the advantages you gain by pausing and the dangers involved with total spontaneity.

The first reason to pause, and the reason most likely to be on your attorney's mind, is that it provides an opportunity for your lawyer to object to the question. If you don't pause, you run the danger of supplying an answer before your attorney has the opportunity to state an important objection on the record.

Pausing gives your lawyer time to object.

The following is an example of a witness who forgot her attorney's preparatory instructions. Read this the way it happened, without pauses:

Q. Prior to this accident, did you ever have any problems with headaches?
A. I still got them.
Q. Prior to—before the accident?
A. Oh, no.
Q. You still have problems with headaches now?
A. Yes.
Q. How often?
A. Lots.
Q. Well, is it more than once a week?
A. Oh, yes.
Q. More than twice a week?
A. I got quite a lot of headaches. It's more than twice a week, yes, more often.
Q. Did you ever tell Dr. Hagman about your having a nervous breakdown?
A. No
WITNESS'S ATTORNEY: I object to this line of questioning as being irrelevant.
QUESTIONING ATTORNEY: She's already answered. Were you hospitalized once for a nervous breakdown?
THE WITNESS: Yes.
WITNESS'S ATTORNEY: Don't answer that—Well, too late.

This is an example of a witness who was caught up in the rhythm of the testimony. This actually happened toward the end of a long deposition, where, after question-answer-question-answer, the witness became used to the situation and was willing to answer just about anything. To the dismay of her attorney, the answers quickened as the deposition wore on and the witness's patience wore thin. Her attorney was trying to stop the opposition from encroaching upon a sensitive area. The opposition was trying to gain what the witness's attorney considered irrelevant and possibly damaging information. Although the information may have been technically irrelevant, at least for purposes of a trial, the witness's attorney knew that such information would nevertheless have considerable bearing on the way the opposition viewed the case.

If the witness had taken a moment before speaking, the attorney might have been able to object to the relevancy before the witness testified about not telling important information to her doctor. The witness then compounded the error by giving a further immediate reply to another question on the same topic, before her attorney could blurt out an instruction not to answer.

Pausing before you speak is also the only way to be sure that the interrogator has finished the question. It is human nature to try to anticipate questions. We all have had the experience where, in conversation with someone, we have tried to respond to something being said before the other person has finished speaking. We are especially inclined to do this in a conversation where we feel vulnerable or under attack. Sometimes we find that we guessed wrong about what the other person was about to say. In conversation, although considered slightly rude, anticipating what the other person is about to say and interrupting is usually a pretty harmless mistake. Generally, the other person will indignantly correct the misconception, and then go on to complete the intended thought. At a deposition, the danger of interrupting is that you may accidentally volunteer information by incorrectly assuming you know what the interrogator is after. In other words, you may be supplying an answer to a question that might never have been asked if you hadn't suggested the topic. The interrogator may then follow up on your answer with an entirely different line of questioning before returning to the question originally intended.

> **Pausing gives the questioner time to finish and you time to be sure you answer the question asked.**

There is a third, equally important, reason to pause before you speak. Pausing gives you the opportunity to think about what you are about to say before you say it. Don't forget, your main purpose at the deposition is to make the record. You want to make every effort to be clear, while at the same time answering in as few words as you can, so as not to volunteer additional information.

> **Pausing lets you plan your words.**

Nobody should hurry through an examination before trial. There should be plenty of time to consider your answers before you speak. The record does not show how much time elapsed between the end of the question and the first word spoken in the answer. You could sit there in silence for days (although I wouldn't recommend trying it), and the transcript would still just show the questions and answers following each other. Pausing also helps you, as the witness, to gain some control over the proceedings. It is harder for an antagonistic interrogator to browbeat a witness who maintains this type of control and spaces out the time before the next question can be asked.

One word of caution. I had an experience where a witness took an inordinately long time to answer each question. Either his attorney had overprepared him, or he didn't quite grasp the concept. He took extremely long pauses before answering the simplest questions. I finally tried to faze him by timing one of his pauses. I then asked him, on the record: "It took you one minute and fifty seconds to answer that question. Is there some particular reason why it took you so long to answer?" About a minute later he said, "No."

I continued to occasionally make a record of the length of time between pauses, until his attorney objected a number of times and then, finally, conducted an off-the-record conference, to tell the witness to speed things up. He told his client, "Being careful is okay, but these are, after all, routine questions." The witness then became more confused and fell into the trap of spontaneity. He eventually stopped taking pauses altogether.

Later, at a pretrial settlement conference, I told the judge that I suspected this witness, a party to the lawsuit, was being dishonest because he took so long to answer my questions—and that I intended to bring this to the attention of the jury since it was adequately documented on the record.

The case never got as far as a trial, and I don't know if the judge would have let me use the deposition record to reflect on the veracity of the witness, but I believe that the manner in which the record of testimony came out may have given me some leverage to eventually get the case settled. The moral to the story is that constantly taking extraordinarily long pauses before answering will not help to give the appearance that you are a truthful, straightforward witness with nothing to hide.

While hesitation in daily conversation may give the impression that you are unsure of the answer, short periods of hesitation before speaking at a deposition usually give the impression that you are making an effort to be accurate. A short pause, for a few seconds, to organize your thoughts after each question, should be sufficient.

RULE 2: SPEAK CLEARLY AND SLOWLY

Speaking clearly and slowly at a deposition isn't nearly as easy as it sounds. This also takes a little concentration. Because deponents tend to treat the deposition like a conversation after a while, instead of giving testimony, they often start to merely give replys.

By definition, when you give testimony, you are supposed to give a formal, solemn declaration under oath. A reply should not be a reaction to the interrogator's questions or comments.

Nodding or shaking your head is a reply. Saying "uh-huh" or "uh-uh" is a reply. These are meaningless communications in the realm of the deposition because they are not declarative formal statements to be taken down as part of the record.

Usually, the interrogator will not accept these kinds of answers because it would be too easy for the witness to claim later that the answer was misunderstood. In addition, because the court reporter can't take down a head nod, a sharp reporter will sometimes interrupt the proceedings and ask the witness, "Was that a yes or no?" This can be very disconcerting when you're trying to concentrate on the testimony.

Most of the time, nods and grunts do not become part of the record. An attorney who has lapsed into the same conversational mode as the witness might occasionally let a gap in the testimony go by, only to realize later that an important answer is missing from the record. The attorney may know what the witness meant to say, but not be able to prove what was said because the right words don't appear in the transcript.

In addition to avoiding head nods and grunting or guttural noises as answers, speaking clearly involves taking the time to be sure your brain is in gear before starting your mouth. In other words, try to avoid slurring words and stumbles that may be confusing as part of the record.

If you observe people's everyday speech patterns, you will find that gestures play a big role in communication. But gestures cannot be taken down by the court reporter. The stenographer may write the word "indicating," to show that some response was made, but she will not interpret the gesture. Even though the reporter may know what is being referred to, unless told to do otherwise, "indicating" is all that the reporter will put into the record. If we are sitting in a room together, you may say "It's this long" and show what you mean by gesturing with your fingers, hands, or arms. But for the purposes of a deposition transcript, an answer like "It's this long" could mean just about anything, and therefore means nothing.

Speaking clearly also means avoiding bad speech habits such as putting your hand in front of your mouth, or putting your head down. It also means speaking loudly enough to permit everyone in the room to hear what you are saying. It means not chewing gum, not

Don't nod, gesture, or answer casually. Remember, this is a formal record.

mumbling, and not speaking while you are taking a sip from your coffee cup.

Pity the poor court reporter who has to strain to catch what the witness says. It's very disconcerting to suddenly have the court reporter asking, "What did you say," and have to repeat your answer, word-for-word, if you can. This is one of the reasons why most court reporters prefer to have the witness sit facing them. It is easier for the reporter to tell what a shy or quiet witness is saying if the reporter can watch the movements of the witness's mouth.

As you testify, clarify any confusing terms or names.

The courtesy involved in speaking clearly may also include being prepared to avoid obviously unintelligible testimony. Be prepared to spell technical or confusing words, and be prepared to clarify terms that you know will be misunderstood:

Q. What was the Manager, Bob's last name?
A. Askem
Q. The Manager's name?
A. Askem
Q. He's not here, I'm asking you.
A. I know, his name is Askem. A-S-K-E-M. Askem is his name. I'm not trying to be funny here.

Speaking slowly does not mean it is necessary to speak ultra-slow. The reporter can keep up with what is being said, as long as you don't speak too rapidly. Pick a nice comfortable pace and try to maintain it, even if you get into a heated discussion with the interrogating attorney. It is also helpful to the reporter if you pause once in a while to be sure the reporter has enough time to take down your answer. Pacing your testimony is one more way that you can personally exercise some control over the proceedings. The tempo of your testimony, combined with short pauses before answering, can be used to prevent the interrogator from rushing you, putting pressure on you, or getting you into a combative mode.

RULE 3: BE SURE YOU UNDERSTAND THE QUESTION

If you're not completely sure what you're being asked, don't even attempt to answer. An answer should only be given when the question is fully understood. A deponent who tries to answer without fully grasping the subject of the question takes a tremendous risk.

In order to lock in the testimony for use at trial, it is common practice for the examining attorney to give the witness some preliminary instructions, which are recorded in the transcript:

> Q. Wr. Whimper, my name is Stuart Shapiro. I'm the attorney representing XYZ Corporation in this lawsuit. We're here to ask you some questions about what happened. Do you understand that everything you say in this room will be taken down by the court reporter?
>
> A. I do.
>
> Q. You also understand that you have given an oath to tell the truth and your answers here today should be the same as if you were testifying in court in front of a judge and jury?
>
> A. Yes.
>
> Q. If you don't understand one of my questions, please ask me and I'll rephrase it. If you don't hear something I ask you, please indicate that you did not hear, and I'll repeat it. Fair enough?
>
> A. All right.
>
> Q. Unless you indicate that you don't understand the question, we'll assume for the record that you understood what was asked. All right?
>
> A. Okay.

There are several reasons why you may not understand a question that have nothing to do with your intelligence: There may have been a distraction or some other lapse in your ability to pay attention when the question was asked; the question itself may be complicated or unclear, or may contain so many parts that you don't know which part is to be answered; the attorney may be using a word or phrase that isn't familiar or that has more than one meaning; you may simply have been unable to hear the question.

If you don't hear or don't understand a question, it is up to you to ask to have it repeated. The attorney who asked the question will either repeat it, or will ask the reporter to read it back. This is a common occurrence at depositions, and you should not be embarrassed to admit to missing a question or two.

If you miss or don't understand a question, ask.

If the question is unclear because it is awkwardly phrased, you should ask the attorney to clarify or rephrase it. Never try to guess and respond with what you think the attorney may be looking for. If you try to guess what the attorney has in mind, you may accidentally volunteer information and provide the opposition with testimony on subjects that they would never have thought of exploring:

> Q. How long was the cast on your arm?
> A. About six weeks. I took it off myself.
> Q. Okay, but I'm asking how long it was.
> A. Oh, how long it was, I thought you meant—
> WITNESS'S ATTORNEY: He's asking what it looked like. Where did it go—from your wrist up to past your elbow?
> THE WITNESS: Yes.
> EXAMINING ATTORNEY: Now, you say you took it off by yourself, after six weeks. Did any doctor tell you it was okay to take it off?

Don't try to antici-pate a question; wait for the attor-ney to finish.

The witness must also be careful not to try to be helpful or to out-fox questioners by guessing their objective. Experienced litigators know that they have to be careful to assure that their witnesses understand precisely what the question involves.

> Q. Mr. Curly, has your prescription for eyeglasses been changed recently?
> A. Yes.
> Q. When was it changed last?
> A. About six months ago. I am going to Doctor—
> WITNESS'S ATTORNEY: Please listen to the question.
> EXAMINING ATTORNEY: Do you have plans to see the doctor?
> WITNESS'S ATTORNEY: Which doctor?
> EXAMINING ATTORNEY: What doctor is it?
> WITNESS'S ATTORNEY: Which doctor?
> THE WITNESS: Which doctor?
> EXAMINING ATTORNEY: Do you have plans to see a witch doctor?
> WITNESS'S ATTORNEY: A witch doctor? Do you have plans to see a witch doctor?

THE WITNESS: No. I go to Doctor Howard now, because Dr. Fine sent me to see him. He's no witch doctor. He has an ugly nurse working for him though.

It is very dangerous to try to help the questioner phrase the questions. Most deponents, in an effort to be cooperative, find themselves tempted to offer such assistance. However, you must always avoid the temptation to help the interrogator make up the question.

Even just suggesting words to the interrogator is extremely risky. You may not only suggest something that the lawyer wouldn't have thought about, you may also confuse the record by seeming to answer the questions when you're really just trying to help out:

Q. There were two impacts, correct?

A. That's correct.

Q. Now did both impacts occur at the—

A. Simultaneously.

WITNESS'S ATTORNEY: Well, I'll object to the form.

EXAMINING ATTORNEY: Okay.

THE WITNESS: I don't know.

EXAMINING ATTORNEY: You don't know. Either they did or they didn't?

A. I just said I don't know.

Q. You gave me two answers. You said simultaneously?

A. I was asking you a question, if you meant simultaneously.

Q. Simultaneously was your word, I'm asking the questions here—

WITNESS'S ATTORNEY: Bill, we're not going to play games here on the record. When he said the word simultaneously, he said it with a rising inflection in his voice. He obviously wasn't making a statement. Ask a proper question. I'm not going to have you go back at some point with the transcript and try to nail him down to having said the word simultaneously as being his answer. Now if you want to ask him whether he knows at this point whether the vehicles hit at the same time, I'll allow that question.

EXAMINING ATTORNEY: Sure, that's the question?

THE WITNESS: Would you like to start over?

Q. Sure. Did both the police vehicle and the Westbound vehicle hit your vehicle at the same time?

A. I don't know.

Lawyers usually make up the majority of their questions as they go along. They do this because they don't know what areas to explore in depth until they hear some of the answers to the basic, preliminary questions. In the attempt to invent questions spontaneously, they sometimes ask questions that are compound or very complex.

If the question is overly complex, ask to have it rephrased.

Complex questions usually involve long hypotheticals. You may be required to consider many intricate details before giving an answer. If asked such a complex questions, be careful that you understand all of the assumptions the questioner is making. If you don't follow the question completely, or if you feel that the question is too complex to answer in the form it is first asked, the best thing to do is simply to ask the questioner to "Please rephrase that."

Another type of complex question involves a double or triple negative. In phrasing the question, the attorney may use several negative words that add up to make the question tricky:

Q. You did not neglect to notify the office when you arrived, did you?

The words "did not" and "neglect" are both negative. If you answer by saying "yes," you are saying you did notify the office. If you say "no," you are saying you neglected to do it. It is easy to see how confusing these questions can be. This is one of the rare exceptions where you should answer a yes-or-no question by saying more than "yes" or "no." To be sure of giving the correct answer, a better response would be to say, "I notified" or "I did not notify the office."

Another type of tricky question is a compound question. A compound question is really several questions lumped together. The danger in attempting to answer compound questions is that you may end up answering only one part of the question and may not remember all that is being asked.

Even worse, one of the attorneys may interrupt your train of thought to pursue the answer you gave to part of the compound question, and you may never get the chance to come back to the original question and answer all of it. The best way to treat a compound question is to pin down the questioner to only one question at a time. A simple rebuff, such as "Which part do you want me to answer first?" is usually enough to make the attorney start over and separate out the individual questions.

If you have any doubt in your mind at all, follow the rule not to answer until you know you fully understand what you're being asked. Some attorneys just don't know how to properly ask a question at a deposition, and a witness has the right to clarity.

From the attorney's perspective, the questioner will be happier in the long run with a record that is clear, so that there can be no argument later about whether you and the lawyer were on the same wavelength. From your point of view, you can exercise enough control over the proceedings to force the questioner to ask clear and concise questions. In this way you won't be trapped into giving improper testimony, whether the trap is intentional or inadvertent.

30

THE OBJECTIVE OF OBJECTIONS

During the course of the deposition, the various lawyers may speak up from time to time and voice certain *objections*. When this happens, be silent and listen carefully to the objection being made and to any response from your own attorney.

An attorney must state objections during the course of the testimony for several reasons. The most obvious reason is to have the objection preserved on the record so that it can be brought to the attention of the court if the case comes to trial. If one of the parties attempts to use the deposition transcript as evidence, the court will review the objections made during the examination, and then rule on whether the evidence is permissible.

On a less obvious level, a lawyer may start raising objections for strategic reasons. Your lawyer may object just to test the legal skills of the opposing lawyer, or to show that you will not be intimidated by unfair questioning or tactics, or to buy time.

For instance, a lawyer may object to questions that are needlessly repetitious. If the question has already been asked in some other form, it is not necessary to answer it again. By raising a timely objection, the lawyer can shorten the deposition and, at the same time, avoid the risk that the witness will give an answer that is inconsistent.

A lawyer may object to questions that are overly broad or that probe into matters that are completely irrelevant to the case. Objections are also appropriate if there isn't a proper foundation for the question,

Stop immediately if your attorney raises an objection, and stay quiet until your lawyer tells you to proceed.

because the subject matter hasn't been covered well enough for the witness to know exactly what is at issue.

An objection may also be made if a question is speculative in nature. A witness cannot be required to give an answer that requires guessing. Objections will also be made if the witness is not qualified to give the answer.

Some questions are objectionable on the basis that the information sought is privileged. For example, the law recognizes certain prior communications that do not have to be revealed during a civil lawsuit, because there is a right to privacy. A question may be objectionable if it requires the witness to reveal communications with a personal physician or private attorney.

Further objections may be raised to prevent the questioner from arguing with the witness, or when the witness is obviously being harrassed by inappropriate questioning.

Your attorney might raise an objection to try to tip you off to a potential pitfall that might arise when framing the answer to a particular question. It is very important to listen to the way these objections are stated because your attorney may go so far as to elaborate upon the objection in a manner that suggests the appropriate answer:

Q. Okay. Now, have you ever heard anyone criticize—any doctor, criticize the care that was given to you by Dr. MacAbre in this case?

A. Has any doctor?

Q. Any doctor?

A. No.

Q. Or have you ever seen a report by any doctor criticizing Dr. MacAbre in this case?

WITNESS'S ATTORNEY: Object to the question. Don't answer it.

EXAMINING ATTORNEY: On what grounds?

WITNESS'S ATTORNEY: Because you may be talking about a report developed for litigation purposes which is privileged, and besides, Roseanne [the client], I don't think you ever actually saw any reports, I don't think you actually saw them.

EXAMINING ATTORNEY: Oh, geez.

WITNESS'S ATTORNEY: I don't think anything was shown to you in the way of written reports. Go ahead and answer the question.

THE WITNESS: No, I haven't seen any reports.

The most common objection made during an examination before trial is an *objection to the form of the question*. This objection combines all of the usual purposes. It is not only an objection that must be preserved on the record for the judge to rule on later; it is also used to tip off the witness, and to tell the attorney who asked the question that there was something wrong with the way it was asked.

It your attorney makes an objection to *form*, it is usually because your attorney wants to be sure you completely understand the question, or to be sure the question can be answered properly the way it is phrased.

The types of questions that are most commonly objectionable on the basis of form are:

- Questions that use a confusing term that may not have the same meaning to everyone
- Questions that assume a fact at issue
- Compound questions that are really several questions combined
- Questions that are so long or so awkwardly worded as to be confusing

When you hear one of the attorneys make an objection to the form of the question, you should immediately stop and take the hint. There could be something misleading or tricky about the question, and special care is required before giving an answer.

Listen to the objection and take the hint to be careful.

Remember, it is preferable to pin down the questioner and to make sure that the question is completely understood before you provide an answer.

31

FIGHTING EBT FATIGUE

A long deposition can be challenging physically as well as mentally. When more than one party is deposed, all the witnesses may be required to attend on the same day. You may have to sit around for a considerable period of time and wait until other witnesses have testified.

A smart witness will come to the examination before trial physically prepared. Avoid staying up late on the night before the deposition. Avoid taking drugs or drinking alcohol, and dress comfortably.

Even the most well prepared witness will suffer some physical strain if forced to sit and listen for several hours before testifying. Most of the testimony is somewhat boring in nature, and usually you can do nothing but sit in an uncomfortable chair and listen, and try to stay with it.

If you have to testify first, the situation changes to one in which you are under increased tension for a long period of time. Maintaining a high level of mental alertness for a long period is also exhausting. You may find that you have trouble paying attention to the witnesses who testify after you.

Attorneys know that a long deposition can be a grueling experience for the witness, and they sometimes try to use this factor to strategic advantage. Some lawyers hold off the questions on important matters until later in the deposition, when they sense that the witness may be starting to tire or become frustrated. At that point, the witness is more likely to forget the warnings received during the preparation session and fall prey to offensive tactics.

Because it is so important to stay sharp and handle the questions cautiously, you must be on your guard for signs of fatigue, and you must know how to deal with it when it arises. Some of the usual signs to watch for include:

Be prepared for a long, stressful session; rest up and watch for signs of fatigue.

- Difficulty listening
- Increased blinking or dry itchy eyes
- Questions starting to lose their meaning as the words don't make sense
- Your body starting to send signals, such as back or leg aches
- Yawning
- Dry mouth
- Headaches
- Slurring your words

At a trial, you might not have the opportunity to take a break. At an examination before trial, you probably can. However, before you ask to take a break, consider this: You are being tested as a witness. Do you want the opposition to think that they can break you down by keeping you on the stand for a long time?

You can do things at the deposition to deal with fatigue, other than taking a recess. Move your head slowly from side to side, so as not to give yourself away. Establish a picture in your mind that you are taking a step back from the proceedings, and try to look at the situation through different eyes.

Another helpful mental image used by many witnesses is to imagine that you are gently pushing back the lawyer who is asking you the questions. Lean a little forward and force yourself to get more involved.

Try to re-energize when you feel fatigue coming on.

If none of those things work, gently squeeze your earlobe, or kick off one of your shoes. Some people gently bite down on the side of their tongues, or squeeze their hands. You may sit up, and take a deep breath, or stretch. Roll your head and ease the tension in your neck. Stand up and remove your jacket. Do what you feel is necessary to get comfortable again, but try to do it without fidgeting or making your discomfort obvious.

If it hasn't already been provided, you may also ask to have a drink of water or a cup of coffee brought to the deposition room. You may even want to bring your own thermos of tea or can of soda if you expect the deposition to last a long time.

The important thing is that you be wary of fatigue and be careful that you are not giving in to it. Go to the deposition prepared for fatigue. Expect it, and, if it appears, do something to re-energize.

32

THE END MAY BE ONLY THE BEGINNING

Witnesses invariably heave a sigh of relief when the examination before trial is ended. They're glad it's over with, not realizing that, as the saying goes, "It ain't over until it's over."

At the end of the deposition, be mindful of the fact that you are still on display. Don't make the mistake of making comments while the opposition lawyers are still within earshot. Don't think that just because the court reporter is putting away the machine, your comments will be off the record. Anything you say can become part of the lawsuit. Your comment may be noted in the opposition's file for later use, even if it isn't part of the transcript of your testimony.

Maintain your composure and your silence as you leave the area.

When leaving the deposition site, try to maintain the same composure you had when you arrived. The overall impression is important.

I recall one case of alleged personal injury in which the plaintiff got up and started to leave the room without taking his cane. His attorney suddenly noticed, and reminded the plaintiff that he'd better "take that along." Needless to say, some questions were raised about whether the witness was exaggerating the extent of his injury. He had been leaning on the cane when he walked into the room, and very few miracles of healing take place during the course of a deposition.

Most witnesses leave the deposition room with some hard feelings about the opposing attorneys and the other witnesses. This is not surprising. Such feelings are natural after an adversarial event. In other words, after what amounts to a polite war, everyone feels at least a little put off. It is a mistake, however, to give vent to these feelings or display them in any way in front of the opposition.

Whether you think that the deposition went well or not, it is only one of several steps in bringing the case to a close. Much more may be needed before a trial or disposition of the case. Further proceedings may be required, as may further paperwork and, possibly further EBT's.

Whether you are a party to the suit, or an independent witness, there is still the likelihood that you will be called upon in the future for further participation. Even if the deposition is the last of the preliminary proceedings that actually require your participation, the timing of the trial will be controlled by the court and cannot always be predicted. You must keep your attorney advised of your whereabouts.

The lapse time following the deposition provides you with the opportunity to reflect upon what has taken place, and to discuss with appropriate counsel any bothersome issues that have been raised.

33

AFTER THE BALL GAME,
CORRECTING THE REPLAYS

There was one time that I thought I was
wrong, but it turned out that I was mistaken.
Anon.

You've testified at an examination before trial and played the game
to the best of your ability. Now you're stuck with the transcript,
right? Maybe not. Read over the following portion of an actual transcript:

Q. Exhibit number 10 and Exhibit number 11 are both photographs. I am going to show you Exhibit number 10 first.
Do you recognize—can you tell me what this is a photograph of?

A. Of a safe design.

Q. Is that—does that safe design come with the machine?

A. No.

Q. Does that safe design, is that put up at the behest of your
field engineer? Do you know?

A. No.

Q. Okay. Have you ever seen a safe design like that one
before?

A. Similar ones.

Q. Okay, in different factories where these kinds of machines
are?

A. Yes.

Q. Do any of these safe designs that appear in other factories that you are familiar with, appear there as a result of instructions from your company to the consumer?

A. I can't be sure of that.

Now go back and read the same testimony, but, wherever the words "safe design" appear, change the words to "safety sign." As you can see, it changes the meaning of the testimony drastically.

This is an actual example of a horrible error made by a court reporter in transcribing testimony. Instead of the witness testifying about a machine that wasn't safely designed, the witness was actually testifying about a photograph of a safety sign.

This may have happened because the reporter did not hear properly, or could not read the notes when making the transcription. It is also possible that a typist misunderstood the court reporter's dictation when the stenographic notes were read back. Whatever the reason, the deposition transcript is radically incorrect merely because of two words that sound alike.

Reporters have been known to skip folds in their paper and leave out entire pages of testimony. Despite being highly trained and well paid for their services, even the best reporters are distracted at times and make mistakes.

MAKING CORRECTIONS

The previous incident is a perfect example of why the witness is permitted to review and correct the transcript before it becomes a final record. Every witness has the right to read the transcript of his or her testimony and make appropriate changes.

You may be able to make changes in the transcript with proper explanations.

Surprisingly, you may make changes in the form of the testimony, or may go so far as to actually change the substance of what you said. For example, if you incorrectly testified about a particular date, and find out about the mistake before signing the transcript, a correction can be made with a written explanation such as, "Date was stated incorrectly."

The explanation must be provided to the opposition. If there is an objection to permitting the correction, it may be necessary for the parties to appear in court and have the judge determine whether the correction is appropriate.

You may go beyond just correcting typographical errors and, if your memory has improved since the deposition, correct an answer that was wrong or incomplete. In other words, you can go so far as to change the testimony from "The light was green" to "The light was red."

Corrections to be made are usually noted on a separate correction sheet, along with the explanation of the reason for the change. A copy of the correction sheet must be provided to each of the attorneys. In this way, all counsel are notified of the corrections in case there is a formal objection to be made. If nobody objects, the correction sheet will usually travel with the completed transcript.

Once the correction process is completed, or, if no corrections are necessary, you will sign the transcript to indicate that it is satisfactory. Your signature is then witnessed or notarized.

Don't take the ability to make corrections for granted. If you make a correction that fundamentally changes the substance of your testimony, the opposition may call you back for a further deposition to ask additional questions about the subject of the change. An opposing attorney may also make comments at trial about the corrections that were made: "Mr. Witness, you first testified that the light was green, and then, after thinking about it, you changed your testimony to the light was red. . . ." This possible commentary brings up the question of whether you necessarily want to correct every minor flaw in the transcript.

WHEN NOT TO CORRECT

What if you find a minor typo and make a correction, but miss a major mistake? It is hard to argue at the time of trial that the transcript is incorrect if you have made other corrections before signing. The opposing attorney will point out that you not only made the statement at the deposition, but failed to change it after reading the transcript, even though other changes were made. On the other hand, if no corrections are made, you still have the option of at least trying to argue that you didn't examine the transcript carefully before signing. Under the right circumstances, it can work to your advantage if you don't make any corrections. Even though minor flaws exist, making corrections is a judgment call that should be discussed with your attorney.

You may not want to correct minor points; discuss the advantages and disadvantages with your attorney.

This is a typical errata sheet used for making corrections to the transcript.

PLEASE ATTACH TO THE DEPOSITION OF _____

IN THE CASE OF _____

_____

ERRATA SHEET

Instructions:

Please read the original transcript of your deposition and make note of any errors in transcription on this page. Do *not* mark on the original transcript itself. Please sign and date this sheet and sign the transcript on page _____. Then kindly return both sheet and transcript to the court reporter whose name is below. Thank you.

Page	Line	Error or Amendment	Reason for Change
93	22	change "safe design" to "safety sign"	testimony misunderstood
145	8	change "my writing" to "not my handwriting"	misunderstood question

I have read the original transcript and, except for any corrections or amendments noted above, I hereby subscribe to the transcript as an accurate record of the statements made by me.

Signature of Deponent: _____

Date: _____ Witness: _____

I have consulted my stenographic notes and agree to the changes initialed by me.

_____

(Reporter)

FINALIZING THE TRANSCRIPT

Two final words of warning. First, depending upon the jurisdiction, there may be a time limit within which to correct, sign, and return the transcript. Florida, for example, does not limit the time unless the parties place a time limit themselves. On the other hand, Alaska, Arkansas, California, Delaware, the District of Columbia, and Hawaii have been known to have 30-day time limits. If signing and correcting is not accomplished within 30 days, the transcript stands as is.

Second, before the deposition is finished, you may have to request the opportunity to make corrections. On occasion, the attorney representing the witness may waive the right to sign the transcript. This may be done because of convenience or time limitations, or for some other reason (such as the attorney doesn't consider the case to be serious enough to warrant the extra work). The attorney may also be trying to send the opposition a message of fearless resolve.

Signing and correcting the transcript is a right held by the witness. Unfortunately, very often, the witness is not consulted before the attorney agrees to waive the signing. In fact, the stipulation may be entered at the beginning of the deposition, and the witness may not even be aware of it. Woe to the witness who cruises through the deposition thinking that mistakes can be corrected later, only to find out that the right to make corrections has unknowingly been waived.

Consult with your attorney **before** the deposition to be sure that you don't waive your rights, or at least be sure you understand the strategy involved.

Before the deposition, discuss with your lawyer any special rules and time limitations on making corrections.

34

VIDEO GAMES

As technology has changed, so have depositions. At one time, all reporting was taken down in shorthand on tablet paper. With the advent of the shorthand machine, court reporters were able to improve speed, efficiency, and accuracy. Modern stenographic machines have computer compatible memory that records testimony in the form of electronic impulses. The impulses are fed to a computer that speeds the process of converting the reporter's notes into a written transcript.

For a while, court reporters were experimenting with voice recorders that required them to wear a microphone that resembled a gas mask and repeat everything they heard into the microphone. Because of the unreliability of early tape recorders, this method usually required a backup system, using another recorder and microphones placed around the room. The burden of utilizing all of this equipment for the purpose of eventually creating a written transcript made this method unpopular.

Each new improvement has the burden of proving its trustworthiness over time. It must be shown to be a reliable tool for the presentation of evidence to the court. Each new recording method undergoes a period of experimentation, is scrutinized by the courts, becomes standardized, and eventually becomes old hat.

The technique of presenting videotaped evidence at trial is still in its infancy. In addition to being used to record a deposition, video is now being used to show evidence such as fire damage or the scene of an accident; to show a typical "day in the life" of the victim; or to record the testimony of a child to spare the child the trauma of sitting on a witness stand in open court.

BENEFITS OF VIDEO

Although video depositions are currently the exception rather than the rule, there are several reasons for video tape recording an examination before trial.

To make a particular impression a videotaped deposition may be preferred to a dry transcript of a witness who won't be able to appear in court.

Video can be used to capture the testimony of a witness who will not be available to appear at the trial in person. Lawyers give substantial consideration to how the demeanor of a particular witness will affect the case. Given the choice of merely reading to the jury from a dull transcript or showing a tape of the witness's actual testimony, showing the tape may be greatly advantageous. This is especially true if the appearance of the witness will lend more weight to what is said.

There is also a distinct advantage for the judge, who often has to rule on the validity of certain questions and answers before the deposition testimony is presented to the jury. By viewing a videotape, the judge can minimize the possibility of misinterpreting what actually went on in the deposition room, and can avoid inherent problems in trying to pass judgment upon a cold written transcript.

A witness would naturally find it hard to weasel out of being impeached at trial if there is a video record of the testimony. Trying to claim that the question was misunderstood or that the answer is being misinterpreted won't work when the video can be played back to show the exact context in which the question and answer took place. The video will also show the vocal inflections, facial expressions, and body language of the witness at the exact moment the answer was given, making the testimony harder to disclaim.

DRAWBACKS TO VIDEO

There are several potential drawbacks to making a video deposition. One of the prime considerations is that it is much more expensive to conduct a video deposition. Elaborate equipment is required for the taping, and it is difficult and expensive to set the tape up for playback in the courtroom.

It is also harder to pick and choose portions of video testimony if the entire tape isn't played during trial. When reading from a written transcript, the lawyer simply picks and chooses the portions pertinent for the jury to hear. To present video testimony, arrangements must be made for the screen to go blank and for the tape to be fast-forwarded to precisely the right spot to play back the pertinent portions.

Courts have not yet answered the problem of how to go about affording a video witness the opportunity to correct testimony. Do you go back and retape? If the court merely deletes portions of testimony from the video, then there may be no testimony at all concerning certain subjects. The answer may be to have the video witness waive the privilege of correcting the testimony. After all, a witness on the stand at trial doesn't have the opportunity to go back and review and change testimony.

Of course, the potential for witness impact can work both ways. In addition to presenting an inexorable witness, videotape can be used to capture squirming admissions in their most damaging and effective form. A videotape may present a picture of a witness who is so unconvincing that the words would be better received by a jury if merely read to them by someone else.

Video depositions are more expensive and harder to correct.

POTENTIAL ABUSES

The courts are presently in the process of establishing and reviewing rules to prevent abuse of the video medium and to provide for more effective use of videotape on a more common basis.

One problem that has arisen is that a sharp attorney can use—or misuse—the medium by placing extraneous video impressions before the eyes of the jury. These impressions may act subliminally to greatly affect the impact of the testimony presented.

For example, a few years ago I was involved in defending another personal injury case in which the plaintiff had been hospitalized and treated in Canada. The plaintiff's attorney obtained a court order to allow the testimony of the plaintiff's treating physician to be videotaped in Canada for presentation at the trial in New York.

Upon arriving for the videotaping session at a medical center, I found that the plan was to present the doctor, in his office, behind his desk, with his impressive diplomas mounted on the wall behind him. The potential impact of utilizing such a video image is obvious. It would also be unfair. Certainly, doctors would not be allowed to bring their diplomas into the courtroom and hang them up behind the witness stand.

Fortunately, in this particular instance, we found an excuse to move the deposition to a more neutral setting. There wasn't enough room in the office to seat all of the people comfortably. In addition to the witness, there were two defendants' attorneys, one plaintiff's attorney, a separate Canadian attorney representing the doctor, the video machine operator, a camera operator, and an additional stenographer. In order to find a place where everyone would fit, we moved from the small office to a conference table in another part of the medical center—surrounded by plain walls.

Other games can be played with a video camera that will have a subconscious effect upon the viewer. Most video cameras are equipped with zoom lenses that can be adjusted to close in on a speaking witness. Unfortunately, we have all been subconsciously trained by television and movies that the camera will zoom in on the speaker at the most important points in the dialogue. If the zoom is used during a deposition, it can seem to give added significance to the words spoken by the witness.

To avoid this problem, some jurisdictions have ruled that a deposition must be videotaped with a static camera. No movement of the video image is allowed, except perhaps to photograph evidence that must be seen up close while the witness uses it in the testimony.

The video medium is subject to potential abuse; if you are being taped, watch for suspect camera angles.

Another favorite ploy in video imaging is using camera angles to create an impression. Watching your local news, you will probably notice that the angle of the camera is such that the anchor person is placed upon a pedestal. The viewer appears to be looking at a slight upward angle. Like a child who looks up to its mother or father or a class that looks up to the teacher, an impression of authority can be given to almost any witness by adjusting the camera angle so that the witness is on a higher level. Conversely, the impact of a witness can be minimized by shooting at a downward angle. If the situation calls for it, the camera can be used to create the impression that the witness is an average, straightforward, honest person, by shooting so that the camera is on the same level and looks straight into the witness's eyes.

Video also introduces the element of a soundtrack into the situation. In reviewing the videotape of the Canadian doctor taken at the medical center, we suddenly noticed the sound of a siren in the background. It occurred right as the doctor began to speak about his first contact with the patient in a hospital emergency room. The potential to use the soundtrack subliminally requires that the entire video be scrutinized before presentation to the jury. Whether intentional or not, fairness requires that nothing but the actual facts and evidence be presented at trial.

On the other hand, most jurors find it extremely boring to watch a video deposition. Watching movies and television has made us used to constantly changing scenes and shots. It is rare to find a single image on television that does not change within five or ten seconds. This conditioning makes it hard for most jurors to view a video deposition of a talking head when the scene does not change for hours.

Because of this, there is the temptation to play with the camera, to zoom in and out, and manipulate the image to present more of a TV show than a mere video transcript. I have yet to see a court case in which a video deposition has been challenged upon these grounds, but with the increasing use of video in the courtroom, it is bound to come up in the near future.

How to Adjust to Video

Because the video camera records everything that is happening in the deposition room, instead of just making a record of the words that are said, much of what applies to giving good testimony at a normal examination before trial is **not** good practice at a video deposition. A video deposition must be treated more like giving testimony in open court.

Different rules of testifying apply to videotaped depositions.

To begin with, as a video witness, you don't have the luxury of pausing for a long period of time to think about what to say. The tape is rolling, and the trial court will be watching how you respond to the question. Not only the time you take to answer, but your voice inflections, speaking speed, facial expressions, and body language become part of the testimony.

Be careful about gesturing. It looks different on the video screen than it does in person. You will also want to avoid making faces or "mugging" for the camera. The nature of a video deposition is that you will probably be photographed from the waist up. The viewer will most likely have a better view of your face on the video monitor than if you were sitting on the witness stand at the other end of a courtroom.

Don't be afraid to look directly at the camera. Shying away from the camera can give the mistaken impression that you are embarrassed or hiding something.

Dress conservatively. Men look better in grey suits. White shirts have a tendency to wash out under the lights. A light-colored shirt is better. Be careful to select an appropriate tie. Beards show up under the scrutiny of the video lense. A close clean shave is best. A full beard should be neatly trimmed.

Women should wear solid colors and avoid busy designs, which look distracting. Light makeup is recommended. The use of necklaces, brooches, and other kinds of jewelry should be minimized or avoided altogether. Such objects tend to reflect light and sparkle and distract on the television screen. All of this, of course, depends on the overall impression you are trying to convey.

Because special bright lights may be needed to make the video, people tend to perspire more. Drink less water and wear dark clothes if you expect this to be a problem.

There will be microphones present. They are sensitive to sounds you wouldn't expect, such as rustling papers or bumping the table. They also pick up your voice if you start thinking out loud or muttering to yourself.

FUTURE USE

It is hard to predict the future use of videotaped testimony. Many litigators feel that video testimony may supplant the written transcript at some point. However, at the present time, many jurisdictions require that a stenographer be present to make a simultaneous written transcript in case something goes wrong with the videotape.

There have already been video depositions transmitted via overseas satellite. Although very expensive, it is now possible through satellite linkups for a witness to be at one location, and to be questioned by attorneys in a TV studio thousands of miles away. In the future, this may reduce travel time and expense for lawyers and witnesses, but at the present time, most lawyers don't favor this kind of setup because it is hard to control what is happening off camera.

35

How to Survive a Deposition—A Quick Review

Read this chapter again, for review, right before you testify. Here, in a nutshell, are the most important rules for giving effective testimony at an EBT. If you follow these rules, you will survive the deposition with the least amount of unnecessary damage:

1. Listen carefully to each question you are asked.
2. Be sure you understand the question. If you don't, pin the questioner down. Obtain clarification on compound questions or terms that are confusing. Don't answer until the question is clear.
3. Answer only the question that is being asked. Don't volunteer information.
4. Pause before you speak. Make sure the questioner is through with the question. Think about what you're going to say before you say it. Give your attorney the opportunity to jump in and object.
5. Give the shortest possible answers. Answer "yes" or "no," or use as few words as you can.
6. Don't guess. If you don't know an answer, or you can't remember the information, don't be afraid to say so.
7. Speak up. Talk loudly enough to be heard clearly. Avoid head nods, gestures, and grunts.

Review these fourteen rules before you testify.

8. Speak slowly and look the questioner in the eyes.
9. Do not make faces or comments while others in the room are testifying.
10. Don't argue—that's a trap.
11. Be sure of any evidence you are shown and identify the particular item you are talking about.
12. Remember, this is a question-and-answer session, not a conversation.
13. Listen to your lawyer's objections, and take the hint.
14. Be patient and take the deposition seriously.

No matter how foolish the proceedings may seem at times, remember that there are potential ramifications to every answer you give. The lawyers who are present are experts in examination before trial. They have strategies at work that may not be readily apparent to you while you are testifying. Follow the list of rules carefully. That's the only way you can be assured of not falling prey to the interrogating lawyer's tricks of the trade.

36

CONCLUSION

The greatest fool may ask more than the wisest man can answer.

C.C. Colton

In the future, our courts will continue to press for the resolution of cases without trials. Sandra Day O'Connor, associate justice of the United States Supreme Court, has said "[The courts of this country] should be the places where disputes end after alternative methods of resolving disputes have been considered and tried." If every lawsuit had to have a trial, our legal system would collapse.

Giving the litigants access to the evidence in advance promotes what the courts refer to as *judicial economy*. It's another way of saying, "Don't waste the court's time." The court saves time if the parties are prepared to conduct an efficient trial. The court saves even more time if the parties don't show up at all.

Although each court's system of discovery varies to some degree, each aims to establish the truth in its most easily presentable form by allowing the parties to get at all of the available evidence. As long as the method of discovery isn't overly burdensome, courts are inclined to grant the parties the opportunity for as much discovery as possible. In the case of depositions, this usually means a fishing expedition in which the witness must answer a multitude of questions on subjects that seem only remotely connected to the lawsuit.

Depositions Are Here to Stay

It is now an accepted premise in legal circles that the best way to establish the facts of a lawsuit is to submit the witnesses to examination before trial. Even the suits that are eventually submitted to arbitration and mediation usually go through discovery and depositions before the parties determine to resolve them. More often than not, successful discovery makes a trial unnecessary.

Nobody can predict exactly what will happen at your deposition. Use what you've learned here, combined with your lawyer's special skills, to prepare for an effective deposition.

Some lawyers still believe that they should be able to gain an advantage by employing secrets of the trade to manipulate the testimony of witnesses. This book was written to give you an advantage by giving away some of the usual tricks lawyers use to make or destroy a case during depositions. This book is an important step, made necessary by the increasing emphasis on depositions as a routine aspect of litigation. However, to be truly effective at an examination before trial, it's going to take a team effort. You must work closely with your lawyer, using the knowledge imparted here in conjunction with your lawyer's special preparation techniques, because every case will be different. You must consider the distinctive aspects of your particular litigation, and thoroughly prepare using all of the available methods and information.

Depositions are a fascinating aspect of our legal system because nobody can predict exactly what will happen when a group of near strangers get together in a room to ask and answer questions. However, whether you are a party to the litigation, an independent witness, or an expert employed for the occasion, the examination before trial is an extremely important legal proceeding. It warrants taking the time to be as prepared as possible.

My hope is that, by showing you certain of the secret weapons that lawyers are prone to use during an examination before trial, the end result will be to help you, and the legal system in general, in the often burdensome quest for truth and fairness.

INDEX